HIGHLAND MEMORIES

HIGHLAND MEMORIES

BY

COLIN MACDONALD

AUTHOR OF "ECHOES OF THE GLEN"
"HIGHLAND JOURNEY" AND "CROFT
AND CEILIDH"

THE MORAY PRESS
EDINBURGH & LONDON

FIRST PUBLISHED 1949

PUBLISHED BY THE MORAY PRESS, 57 GEORGE ST., EDINBURGH
AND 54 BLOOMSBURY ST., LONDON, W.C. I

PRINTED BY THE DARIEN PRESS LTD., EDINBURGH

CONTENTS

CHAPTER I

CHAPTER IX

CHAPTER X

CHAPTER XI

CHAPTER XII

CHAPTER XIII
(*Being Extracts from Diary*)

CHAPTER XIV
(*Being Extracts from Diary*)

CHAPTER XV

CHAPTER I

Lucky Escape

WHEN senility first came creeping up on old Elspeth she used to laugh heartily at her stupid little mistakes; but she began to think the thing was getting beyond a joke when one winter's night she carefully set the hot-water bottle on the door-step, and took to bed with her the milk pitcher carefully rolled in flannel and wondered why she felt so cold.

Well, with that sort of thing in mind, while in process of putting together what is now being irrevocably committed to public exposure, every now and again there would come to me the shattering fear that in trying to write another of my story-books I was merely piling up proof of advancing senility. And as (so it would appear !) I am not yet so far gone as to be quite indifferent, the thought would so effectively scotch all zest for literary achievement as to put the pen idle for days; indeed it might take weeks to recover morale if, during such days of punctured vanity, I found myself putting salt in my tea or, when homeward bound, wondering vaguely why the shops seemed so strangely unfamiliar until I realised my No. 16 car was nearing the Crematorium instead of Morningside Station.

Just to what extent I have managed to conceal evidence of advancing years must be left to readers to decide; but at least I can assure them that in that respect this book is not nearly so bad as the sort of book I was itching to write—and of which indeed I did write several chapters. For I have to admit the sad fact that there is growing within me the foolish ambition to turn preacher.

Looking round on a world of humanity gone stark mad, like Omar I find myself ambitious

> " To grasp this sorry Scheme of Things entire
> And then remould it . . ."

Dash it all! am I not crawling up to the seventy? And in that time isn't any average person bound to have gathered innumerable wrinkles in the art of avoiding trouble? So I wrote what I hoped would be regarded as clever sentences, laughing at the philosophers who had propounded for the guidance of humanity " systems " so profound as to be but vaguely comprehensible to themselves and of no earthly use at all for ordinary people. I listed some of the commoner causes of troubles and from my pharmacopœia of experience prescribed a cure or at least a mitigation for each.

Take matrimony, for instance. In principle one of our best institutions ; but what a gamble as usually approached ! And what a mess it can make of lives ! I was eloquent on the folly of young folks entering so solemn and intimate a state with no firmer foundation for future accord than that provided by the transient and treacherous promptings of wildly beating hearts. I made a list of the less romantic but more stable dictates of commonsense, so desirable when computing the chances of success in the Matrimonial Stakes.

Then on the folly of taking offence, losing one's temper, quarrelling ! Highlanders came in for a special roasting here—the fiery sort of creature who, when called a coward or a cheat or a thief, deems it the first duty of a gentleman to draw dirk or sgian dubh in defence of honour. Honour my foot ! Instead of getting red at the neck and snatching at the sgian dubh, why not consider the charge calmly? If as a result of calm and honest reflection he knows the charge to be true, why should he take offence at being told the truth? On the other hand if it is not true, why not express regret that his accuser should be so misinformed—and smile—and suggest a dram together? And so on through a long list of human follies and failings and stupidities. With modest pride I read some of the best bits to the family critics, savouring on my literary palate the sentiment and style. Their verdict was kindly candid : they didn't approve. . . .

Yet when I got over the first disappointment it became rather obvious that not many would want to live in the dreary tedium of my Utopia. So I again fell back on Omar and decided to

> ". . . leave the Wise to wrangle and with me
> The Quarrel of the Universe let be,"

and make another raid on the recesses of memory for a few stories which may, I hope, help to pass an armchair night.

CHAPTER II

A Study in Languages—A Qualified Stalker

How prone most of us are to think that foreigners who neither speak nor understand our language must of necessity be of a lower grade of intelligence than ourselves! Personally, although I know it is absurd, I can never quite overcome that instinctive assumption—and should therefore be not too critical of our English visitor who, on his first contact with the Highlands, is apt to jump to an equally erroneous conclusion in regard to native Gaelic speakers, who either speak English not at all or only slowly and brokenly and with a Gaelic lilt. True, accounts are squared in that each is under the same misapprehension in regard to his superiority over the other; and many a time have I wished that the " superior " visitor to the Highlands knew just what the seeming-stupid Highlander thinks of *him* and his intelligence! As one with some knowledge of both languages and people, and weighing up the matter without bias, I give it as my opinion that, by and large, there is little difference in the standard of natural intellectual endowment between *Gall* and *Gael* ; but that if there is any difference the superiority lies with the latter. Certainly there is a gift for natural philosophy and a rock-bottom commonsense quality about most Gaels that sometimes is profound to the point of genius. If only I could adequately reproduce in a book or play what happened soon after the first big war at a hearing before an arbiter in Edinburgh, where the principal witnesses were old crofters who had never previously given evidence in any court of law or arbitration, I would make a fortune ! The whole tale is too long to tell here, but I must try to give a sample of some of the high spots.

In that war, as in the next, our food supply was the most vital question. To minimise the danger, drastic powers were given under D.O.R.A. to various Government departments and Ministers. Amongst these was power to authorise the grazing of sheep and cattle on deer-forests and the killing of deer. In the recent war such measures were, in the main, taken for granted and heartily co-operated in by deer-forest owners, but in 1914 so unprecedented an encroachment on the hitherto private and sacrosanct rights of the landowner evoked not a little resentment in certain quarters. But, in accordance with the usual British scrupulous concern for fair play, due regard was had to a right of compensation in respect of any proved loss consequent on the operation of such powers; and it was when an aggrieved deer-forest owner was trying to substantiate before an arbiter in Edinburgh a compensation claim for several thousand pounds that the crofters were brought into the case as witnesses; for it was to them and their neighbours that the right of killing down the deer on this particular forest had been granted.

The case came before an eminent legal gentleman in Edinburgh. It was a full-dress affair of wigs and gowns, with senior and junior Counsel on either side, and might well be thought likely to strike the layman's heart with awe. The Department's solicitor, astutely questing for some advantage which might tend to counteract any inferiority complex which so impressive an occasion might produce in his witnesses, conceived the idea that their evidence should be given in Gaelic and translated by a competent interpreter. With this the witnesses heartily concurred—and this notwithstanding the fact that for two or three years they had conducted a voluminous correspondence with the Department couched in the best of English! They were warned, however, that for the purpose of this hearing they had *no* English.

But as this ruse had not been thought of earlier, and as the case was now due to commence, nothing could be done about having an interpreter there in time for the start. So it was decided that, when the time for evidence-taking came, Department's Counsel would ask permission of the Arbiter to have the crofters' evidence taken in Gaelic. The request was duly submitted, and the Arbiter, obviously somewhat flattered by the rather unusual " tone " which such a proceeding would confer on the case, readily assented. *An duine bochd!* (Poor man!)

Immediately there arose the question of a suitable interpreter. Some of us present who might be otherwise qualified were ruled out as " interested parties," so :

10.30 A.M.—Court adjourned to give opportunity of finding interpreter.

Phoned most likely man in Edinburgh—not at home— gone to Glasgow by morning train.

Phoned two others in succession—not available.

After much phoning got in touch with the man who had gone to Glasgow. He would return early and be available at 2.30 P.M.

11 A.M.—Court resumed.

Report on hunt for interpreter submitted.

Court adjourned till 2.30 P.M.

2.30 P.M.—Court resumed.

The first question seems a simple one, but Eoghan (who understands it perfectly in both languages) must sense a snag, for he asks the interpreter for further elucidation. This is given—generously. Eoghan wants further enlightenment before committing himself to a reply—and more, and still more, so that he and the interpreter have animated exchanges in Gaelic, prolonged for several minutes; and the answer when it does finally come is just " *Tha* " (" Yes ").

The next question necessitates the same cautious approach and produces the same answer. The third requires even more exhaustive study ; but this time Eoghan is able to avoid monotony by giving a firm negative, " *Cha'n eil.*"

4 P.M.—Arbiter beginning to doubt the efficacy of a system of examination and " crossing " which, in an hour and a half of much conversation but monosyllabic replies, does next to nothing towards getting on with the case. Besides, having found amongst his papers a copy of a three year old letter addressed to the Department—and purporting to have been written and signed by Eoghan— his temper is getting frayed at the thought of possible deception. At last he can stand it no longer: he raps his hand on the desk and fixes on Eoghan the stern optic of the law.

" Come, come ! This is just a waste of time. I suspect you have a very good knowledge of the English language? "

He is speaking direct to Eoghan and obviously expects a direct reply. But Eoghan remembers his lesson : he has no English this day. So he turns to the interpreter and asks, " *Ciod e tha e ag ràdh?* " (" What is he saying? ") The interpreter proceeds to enlighten him, but his Honour will have none of it.

" No, no ! We have had enough of this ! Read that " (passing the letter on to Eoghan). " You wrote that letter did you not? "

" *Ciod e tha e ag ràdh?* " Eoghan again asks.

This time the interpreter is allowed to explain; so Eoghan must do something about it. He does. He slowly searches all of his six capacious pockets for his spectacles—which he ultimately finds and adjusts very carefully on his nose. He picks up the letter, has a look

at it, but at once lays it down again. The spectacles nee
wiping. He takes them off, has a prolonged search f(
his big bandanna, breathes audibly on each lens an
polishes it with the hanky. Again the spectacles a
carefully mounted for action and again Eoghan picks u
the letter.

For one devoid of a knowledge of English he looks a
it for quite a long time. Actually he reads every wor(
of it—twice over. Then he lays it down, removes th(
spectacles, lays them reverentially in their polished tin
case—which he deposits in the appropriate pocket—and
turns towards the interpreter. There is an expectant
hush in Court.

" *Abair ris nach do sgriobh mise am print tha sin!* "   (" Tell
him that I didn't write that print!")—What Eoghan has
been reading is only a typed copy of the original letter!

This—after what seemed an hour of waiting—when
interpreted to his Honour fairly gets his Honour's goat.

" I'm not asking if you wrote that print," says he
quite testily.   " I'm asking if that is a copy of a letter—i
very good English—which you wrote to the Department?

But Eoghan is taking no chances on that : the mos
that can be got from him is that he " didn't write tha
print."

So there is nothing for it but a search amongst the
barrow-load of official files for the original letter.   And
as that will be a long job and it is now late in the day, at

5 P.M.—Court adjourned till 10.30 A.M. to-morrow.

NEXT DAY.   10.30 A.M.—Same scene, same actors.

Eoghan is given the original letter.   He goes through
the same elaborate process of cleaning his spectacles,
scrutinising the document and finally putting everything
in its proper place.   Then he cogitates deeply for quite
half a minute.

" Did—you—write—that—letter? "   asks his Honour

rather balefully; which awkward question is duly translated for the witness's benefit.

Eoghan takes a deep breath—" *Cha'n eil mi ag ràdh nach do sgriobh.*" (" I'm not saying that I didn't.")

HIS HONOUR. I am not interested in what you are *not* saying. What I want to know is : did you or did you not write that letter ?

EOGHAN (to interpreter.) " *Ciod e tha e ag ràdh ?* "

Again the interpreter translates the question to which his Honour demands an answer. But the most that Eoghan can be bludgeoned into admitting is " *Feudaigh e bhi gu do sgriobh—ach fhuair mi cobhair.*"

INTERPRETER. My Lord, the answer is: " It may be that I did—but I got help."

HIS HONOUR. Oh ! Who helped you ?

Eoghan duly waits for the translation. He gazes stolidly at the ceiling for quite a while, then searches for and finally finds the big bandanna, buries his face in it, blows a blast like the Misnish fog-horn, returns the hanky to its lair and in most respectful but firm accent:

" *Abair ris (le chead) gur e mo bheachdsa nach eile còir aige air sin fhaighneachd, agus nach fhaod mise freagairt thoirt dha.*" (" Tell him—with respect—that it is my opinion that he has no right to ask that question and that I do not require to answer it.")

A roar of laughter throughout the Court—in which his Honour joins heartily; he frankly admits the correctness of the reply and thoroughly enjoys the joke against himself. Later, on the adjournment for lunch, he compliments Eoghan on his ability as a witness—although admitting his evidence did not further the case much in any direction ! Then says he, " It's a grand language the Gaelic ! Do you know that as a boy in Argyllshire I used to have quite a smattering of Gaelic—but I'm sorry to say I have forgotten most of it."

2

" Chist like me weeth the Eengelish ! " affably agreed Eoghan—his only venture in that language throughout the two days.

.   .   .   .

On the evening of the second day of the deer-forest compensation case the Department's solicitor—while jubilant over the success of his ruse so far—was inclined to be apprehensive as to the wisdom of persisting with it: it might tend to irritate and antagonise the Court to his ultimate disadvantage; and so, after much deliberation he finally decided that the remaining two witnesses must know sufficient English to give their evidence in that language on the morrow: from them the " no English " ban was lifted. Nor was their self-possession and skill in the " box " in the slightest degree impaired by this circumstance.

A strong averment in the Claimant's case was that so many deer had been killed, or died of wounds as a result of inexpert shooting, that the stock of beasts on the forest had been seriously depleted. Seumas, as a crofter and ex-deerstalker had been deputed by the Department to pay a special visit of inspection to the forest in question so that he might be in a position to give expert evidence on the point. He is now giving the appropriate evidence, and is somewhat surprised and not a little hurt that Counsel for Claimant appears to doubt his word. On the contrary, the impudent fellow has actually suggested more than once that Seumas is not telling the truth !— which indignity causes Jimmie to turn red at the collar. But, of course, he must conduct himself as a Highland gentleman : must be patient with this ill-bred person ; so he continues to be calm and polite.

But presumably this is an attitude which Counsel

misinterprets as weakness and indecision, for he continues to press in a most ungentlemanly way the suggestion that, on the occasion of his inspection of the forest, witness must have seen many dead deer and very few living ones. At last witness can stand it no longer: this *creutair* must be put in his place!

" I—wass—not—eenterested—in—dead—deer—and— I—deet—not—see—any. I—was—eenterested—in—the— living—and—I saw—plenty—of—*them*."

It is quite impossible to convey in a book the dignity, deliberation and finality with which this pronouncement was made. Clearly, his last word had been said on the matter. And so Counsel must have sensed, for he dropped it like a hot coal so far as Seumas was concerned.

But later, when Farquhar was giving his evidence, Counsel made another attempt to make capital out of the (allegedly) many deer that had got away wounded as a result of inexpert shooting and subsequently died. He presses Farquhar on the point very hard:

" Did you let many of the deer away wounded? "

Evidently a comparative admission is advisable here:

" Och! a few beasts might get off right enough—*but not so many got away from us as will be getting away from the chentlemen that will be shooting at them.*"

" It's a very difficult matter, is it not, to shoot the proper beasts in the proper way? "

A long reflective pause, then:

" Yiss—but not if you haff knowledge of the work."

" And do *you* claim to have knowledge of the work? "

Very modestly: " Well, I sink I do."

" Ah! You *think* you do, but you are not *sure*? "

Evidently another case of misinterpreted modesty. Through shaggy brows gleam eyes blue and keen as an eagle's, and:

" Well! *If that iss what you are saying!* Feefty years

aco, when I wass a boy, I went ass a gillie for five years at Glencuoich.

" Then I wass under-stalker for other five years.

" Then I wass stalking for ten years at Guisachan.

" After that I wass more than twenty years head-stalker on two of the best forests in the country.

" And I wass a while wiss Maister Weennans.

" And I stalked for two black Preences from India—and for the Grand Tuke Michael—and for King Edward— and for a lot of other pick pucks—*If that is what you are saying!* "

And that was that!

CHAPTER III

Island Cargoes—Coming of the Motor Car

As is the case of all island communities, the most magnetic spot on any of the inhabited islands of the Hebrides is its pier—a *cheithe*; that fascinating centre at which the mail-boat discharges and takes on board its intriguing medley of human beings and merchandise. If only the pier master at any one of these places weren't so engrossed with the doing of his job what rare material for a book couldn't he gather in the course of a year from a systematic noting of the ebb and flow of the life of the community!

To an island people their mail-boat is not merely a structure of hull and masts and funnels and holds: " she " is a veritable sentient thing. On a sunny day and a calm sea, or when the breeze but ruffles the surface so as to catch and reflect the light as in a million mirrors, she is a thing of joy and gladness. When wind and tide combine to rouse to rage seas that threaten to destroy her, for a few awful moments in the trough she creaks and groans in agony—to rise again, trembling and shuddering, but grimly ready for the next round. And so—late indeed it may well be—at long last she rounds the headland to give the anxious watchers on the pier the first sight of her masthead light.

" *Sin agad i! tha i direach air nochdadh!* " (" There she is! she is just showing! ")

And who and what will she bring this time?

As she glides in towards the pier, and while official concern is directed to the sometimes tricky business of getting her safely tied up, there is a sharp exchange of scrutiny between the passengers and folks ashore. Most people are looking for someone in particular; and glad

are the eyes that catch and look into each other, perhaps
for the first time in years; for wide are the wanderings
of the sons and daughters of these islands, and warm,
warm is their welcome home.

But not even sentiment can long stand in the way of
satisfying the robust island curiosity to know what the
boat has brought.

There is an amazing variety of general merchandise,
but certain things catch the eye.   Boxes and boxes of
baker's bread from Glasgow—stale trash compared with
the *aran coirce* and *bonnach eòrna* that their mothers used
to make!

There are bags of carded wool and yarn for the making
of the world-famous *clò* (Harris Tweed) that will help
even *Sasunnaich* to look like ladies and gentlemen!

Large barrels of beer—and wee, wee cases of whisky—
mallachd air an t-àm a th'ann! (that that should be the way
of it!)   That a decent *bodach* cannot get as much of his
native *deòch* as will cheer his heart in the evening of his
day!—that he would have to insult his palate and his
stomach with that trash!   Can you wonder that in the
islands the occasional wreck of a whisky-laden vessel is
ascribed to the benevolence of an all-wise Providence?

The motor car tied on the deck is the subject of considerable conjecture.   Will it be for the hotel—or
doctor—or merchant—or shooting tenant?   But next
moment in some mysterious way the name of Erchie
Chaluim is on every tongue.   Well, well!   Erchie with
a car!   What would his grandfather say if he had lived
to see this day?

Not a bad-looking second-hand either; if he takes care
of that one it will be years before it joins the ever-increas-
ing regiment of derelict cars that bestrew the island's
roadsides.

A Dhia! and do you remember yon day not so many

years ago when the big crowd came to see the steamer
landing the first motor car that was ever on the island—
yon time that the new shooting tenant, not knowing that
he was to make history, decided to bring his car with
him for the shooting season?

The word went round like wild-fire that a " mortar "
was coming by the steamer on a certain day. There was
some apprehension about how the horses would look on
this innovation, but curiosity overcame fear, for when
the great day arrived never was such a gathering of
horses and carts and family parties seen on the pier,
waiting for the boat that was to bring the " mortar."

As per custom, each horse on arrival was solemnly
backed into a place in the pier yard and loused out of
the cart. Then—as per custom—the bit was removed,
a *taod* (rope) tied round his neck and to a spoke of the
wheel, and a sheaf of *arbhar* (corn) placed on the ground
for him to munch, while the family packed on to the pier
to get the first glimpse of the new arrival.

Soon the steamer hove in sight and as she approached
the pier there, sure enough, was the " mortar " tied firmly
on deck !

Like so many things in an island community, due
consideration had been given to the state of the tide;
with the result that when the boat arrived her deck and
the pier were practically on a level. Two strong planks
were laid from pier to deck, and with considerable
shouting and shoving the car was soon on the pier. A
blue-coated brass-buttoned gentleman went to the car,
opened a " lid " near the front of " her " and did something to the inside. Excitement was intense. The man
with the brass buttons inserted a handle in her nose and
" whirled " two or three times. Nothing happened !
Sarcastic doubts were expressed about the possibility of
the contraption ever doing anything. Brass Buttons again

lifted the lid, tickled her inside and again whirled the handle.

" Brrrrrrrrrr——" said the " mortar," and her shaking and trembling like she was alive !

This astounding development caused the crowd on the pier to back so suddenly that two boys near the edge were pushed over into the sea—but quickly scrambled to safety on the under-beams. Soon all eyes and interest were again on the " mortar." The driver, now in his seat, pulled and pushed things, and slowly, very slowly and quietly, without help of horse or man, she began to move forward !

All this had happened in front of a shed which screened that part of the pier from the horses who were happily munching their sheaves round the corner; but when the car went to turn the corner and the driver saw a dense crowd of people still in front of him he suddenly squeezed the rubber bulb, and " Dhoat ! Dhoat ! Dhoat ! " said the " mortar."

Now the horses were accustomed to the ringing of bicycle bells, to the sound of a ship's siren and of the breakers on the rocks ; but this was a new one on them entirely ! On the instant each horse shot his head high into the air—and broke the *taod* that had tied him to the wheel !

Momentarily mesmerised by the sight of a hideous monster creeping stealthily towards them, the horses could only stare in horror. Then another " Dhoat ! " from the car and the spell was broken ! With one accord every horse dashed for the gateway. But the gateway was only nine feet wide and nearly fifty maddened horses were striving to get through it at the same moment. Saddles, breechings and bridles—and even collars and hames—were torn off in the mad scramble. As each horse got clear of the mêlée and pelted off up the road at the gallop he held his head high, turned it this way and that as frightened horses do, and trumpeted his mixed fear and contempt of the awful thing that had come to the island.

The owners' whoa! whoas! were futile in that mad stampede. Not a horse stopped until he reached the safety of his stable—and that in some cases was seventeen miles away. Never was such a scattering of harness. Each man did his best to collect his own, but at the end of two years many a bridle and *briogais* was still missing and some were never recovered.

Gléidh mise! And now the beasts on the island will hardly get up from their siesta on the warm sandy road to let your car pass; the cow, whose granny the sight and sound of the first aeroplane drove frantic from the machair, is annoyed if you disturb her cud-chewing bliss by shooing her away to allow a bomber to land!

CHAPTER IV

Harris Show-day Troubles

We were dead out of luck with the Harris Agricultural Show. It had always been held on the same day of the last week of August. Meteorically its experience had never been too happy, but now, for three years in succession, it seemed that a sinister Weather Clerk had been balefully determined to make clear to the Committee his disapproval of that particular day. His first effort was just bad enough to make show-going unpopular to the extent that there was only about half the usual turnout of people. Next year, as if offended by the Committee's failure to take the hint, he put on a more wrathful turn that left groups of drenched sheep miserably huddled in corners, too dispirited even to chew the cud, while cattle and horses, with tails to the storm, humped their backs and, with a pathetic look in their bright brown eyes, perhaps questioned the sanity of their masters.

At the after-rally in the inn that evening it was generally agreed that there appeared to be a case for considering a change of date; indeed most of the members of the Committee, in informal talks through the ensuing winter, tended to favour the idea. But, when it came to the formal meeting to arrange for the next show, the Committee were badly shaken by Uilleam Thormaid's strongly-voiced prediction that the chances of getting a storm on the same day three years in succession were so remote that their safer course would be to stick to the same old date. And so it was decided. And, to make a painful story short, this year the storm deity really let them have it. He did scurvily, too, in giving them a bonnie morning; so that every person that could walk set off in high glee for the show; the ladies in their lightest and brightest of frocks, and carrying umbrellas or parasols only for that little extra bit of dash so favoured by the feminine mentality. Having thus lured his victims to the stake our sadistic despot proceeded to do his dirty work with a malevolence which soon achieved the complete ruination of a big percentage of all frocks, parasols and umbrellas on the island.

The Agricultural College marquee with its so beautifully arranged display was wrenched from its moorings to come down a sopping, flapping canvas on our heads. Literally a blow-out as well as wash-out of a day, and the reputation of Uilleam Thormaid as a wise man slumped badly.

Next year the decision was prompt and unanimous: that fiend of a week was given the go-by. The Show was fixed for the first week in September.

With a perversity characteristic of Hebridean weather the old Show date turned out to be a beauty of a day: a day of sunshine and singing larks and quiet blue seas. Well, well! However, the portents were good. It was firmly believed that genial conditions would continue for perhaps a fortnight. Certainly it couldn't break by next Wednesday, the new date for the Show.

On the Friday prior to this Wednesday the usual crowd was waiting on Lochmaddy pier for the arrival of the S.S. *Lapwing*, that in those days left Portree every Monday, Wednesday and Friday morning for Harris— Lochmaddy —Dunvegan—Uig, and did the reverse run on Tuesdays, Thursdays and Saturdays. This Friday afternoon we saw her approaching from well out the Minch. The sea was like glass. Soon the *Lapwing* disappeared from our view while passing behind one of the Maddy Rocks—the " dogs " or Maddies which stand sentinel on the loch and give it its name. In a few minutes she would appear again, passing the Maddy. Soon we began to wonder why it was she wasn't yet showing. What on earth was delaying her? She should have shown minutes ago! Ah! Here she comes at last! But excitement and speculation ran high as we saw an obviously crippled *Lapwing* crawling crab-wise towards the pier.

We could see that her bow was bashed in. Her engines didn't have their usual rhythmic beat. The captain stood sphinx-faced on the bridge. Donald MacAskill was wiping his bleeding face with his hanky. It was from Donald we got the first inkling of explanation.

"Talk about a slip between the cup and the lip!" said he with a grin that cracked his face and started the bleeding again. "I was down in the saloon having a last *deoch an doruis* with Erchie. 'Well, well, *slaint*!' said Erchie to me. '*Slainte mhòr*, Erchie' said myself, and me lifting it. But never a taste did I get! I had just got the length of putting the glass to my nose for a sniff when *bang* she went! and the next thing I knew was the tumbler smashing between my face and the mirror, and the stuff in my eyes and running down the outside of my neck. *A Dhia!*"

The story as we gathered it on the pier was to the following effect: The man at the wheel on the *Lapwing* in those days was so stanced that it was impossible for him to get a clear view forward, in consequence of which circumstance he was entirely dependent on the officer on the bridge for steering orders. The previous night the mate of the *Lapwing* had been superintending the loading of cargo and working hard till the early hours of the morning and was consequently so tired that he was momentarily overcome by sleep on the bridge that warm and drowsy afternoon. Normally the ship passed quite close to the Maddy. She was being steered on her usual course. Had the helmsman been in a position to see where the ship was going, he would of course have given the wheel that shade of a turn required on this occasion to counteract the effect of a slight tide drift. As it was, and with no instruction coming from the bridge, instead of just clearing the Maddy, at a speed of some eleven knots the ship hit the rock square on. No wonder Donald's drink went astray!

.   .   .   .

It had been our intention to go from Lochmaddy to Harris by the *Lapwing* the following Tuesday so as to get our demonstration tent and agricultural exhibits all fixed up and ready for the opening of the Show on the Wednesday forenoon. In her crippled state the mail-boat was of course unfit to proceed on her rounds; but that the mishap to her should involve us in any trouble over the ill-fated Harris Show never crossed our minds: we were confident that another boat would be sent to take up the run without delay. So we got all our stuff down to the pier to be ready for the relief boat when she came. But Saturday came and went, and no word of another boat. Sunday—Monday, still no word! We began to get uneasy. We would have to get to Harris by hook or by crook not later than Tuesday evening. Frantic inquiries at the pier and post-office yielded no ray of hope of a relief boat coming in time. Then it was I did one of the most foolish things I have done in my life; and this is how it happened.

Willie Urquhart, the local Excise Officer, was my greatest friend on the island. Although a most efficient Officer of His Majesty's Customs and Excise his special love was reserved for the sea. What he didn't know about boats, big and little, and of every make, wasn't worth knowing. And, as is the way with such experts, he rode his hobby enthusiastically. His 12-foot rowing boat—it also carried a sail—was the smartest thing of its kind. At this time he happened to be courting the lassie who ultimately became his wife, and some of us used to annoy him by arguing in his hearing whether it was the boat or the lassie that held first place in his affections. Actually he was a first-rate boatman and used to do things with his little craft that made ordinary land-lubbers' hair stand on end. Now, a delightful characteristic of the man with a special love of that nature, be it for horse or dog or boat, is his abounding confidence in the object of his affection and in what he can do with it. In an access of such faith and affection my friend had on more than one occasion asserted that, in reasonably fair weather, he would think nothing of sailing his boat from Lochmaddy to Rodil in Harris. As this meant a good twelve miles by sea and included the crossing of the treacherous Sound of Harris—known locally as *Caol an Fhuaim* in reference to its ever-turbulent waters, due to the meeting of opposing tides—I had ventured to doubt the practicability of such an achievement. But of course that merely confirmed him in his faith: that *his* boat couldn't do a thing like that! He would prove it to me some day! It was with this background and the urgent need for getting to the Harris Show that, on the lovely morning of Tuesday, I did that foolish wicked thing.

" Man, Willie," I opened, " there's not a sign of a relief boat yet, and I'm fair stuck for the Harris Show— and it's going to be a grand day ! "

As I had suspected, Willie was far too good a seaman not to appreciate the risks of trying to cross to Harris in so small a boat even on a good day, and if he suspected what I had in mind (as I am pretty sure he did !) the offer which I was angling for didn't come : he merely expressed sympathy with hard luck.

" If only that boat of yours was a bit bigger do you know I believe we could make Rodil of it on a day like this," I goaded.

" My boat is big enough as she is," he bridled, " but I'm to be far too busy here to-day."

" Just that ! " said I most unkindly. " That's what I always thought ! "

" What is it you always thought? " said he challengingly. " Do you think I'm afraid to go? "

" No, no ! " says I; " but you're not going ! you're too busy ! " Even yet I blush at the unfairness of the form of attack.

" Well," quietly retorted my gallant friend and boat lover, " if that's the way of it, I'll go; and we will start from the old pier in two hours from now."

But then it was my courage that failed as I thought of the load we would have on that little craft and of *Caol an Fhuaim*. In addition to a litter of smaller items there were boxes and hampers containing bottled samples of fertilisers and feeding meals; there was a large barrel churn, a wide-legged butter-worker and a cream-separator, as well as a large marquee-tent with poles and furnishing all complete. Then between crew and passengers we were five: Miss Bannatyne, the dairy and poultry expert, John Rose and myself as passengers, and Willie and wee Ewen the stable-boy as skipper and crew respectively. By the time we had piled everything on to the boat it was all too obvious there wasn't going to be much freeboard when passengers and crew got in. Meantime the news that we were setting off for Rodil in the exciseman's wee boat caused consternation in the village. The venture was universally condemned as hare-brained—suicidal ! One friend after another implored us to give it up. In an effort to stop us the hotel lady refused to supply us with sandwiches and beer. The police inspector quite seriously considered whether he should not place us under protective arrest.

Rose entered into the plan in zestful spirit. Miss Bannatyne showed of danger an utter disregard, born of ignorance of it, and of a simple faith in the skill of the superior sex. Personally, but for consideration of loss of face I would gladly have backed out of the whole business; but in any case, even if I had the courage to advise in accordance with the dictates of my now faint heart, such a course would but incur the contempt of the skipper, who was now as one inspired to high adventure. Thus caught in the grip of circumstance, the hotel lady relented and tearfully gave us a bottle of whisky and a generous supply of beer and sandwiches; and off we set at one o'clock of the afternoon.

.   .   .   .

We had already carefully thought out the course and distances and had a neatly prepared time-table. From the old pier to a little beyond the Maddy Rock is a good two miles in an easterly direction. There was hardly a breath of wind, but what little there was came straight from the direction of the Maddy towards the pier. That meant we could not hoist sail till we got clear of the Loch outside the Maddy. We had allowed an hour for rowing out to that point. Then we could hoist sail and get the help of the gentle easterly breeze to waft us along on the straight north-easterly course that would take us to Rodil some ten miles off. We even dared to hope that out in the Minch the breeze might be enough to be of real help, in which case only the helmsman need keep awake; the rest of us could sleep in the sun till we arrived in Rodil about five o'clock. Failing such luck the four men would take spells of rowing in pairs, and at very latest we would be there by six.

Meantime, with Rose and Ewen at the oars, in dead calm we rowed out the narrow channel below the doctor's house and, after clearing the various islets and *sgeirean*, kept her heading straight for midway between the Maddy and Weaver's Point that towers at the north side entrance to the loch; from there it would be literally plain sailing.

But—as so often happens!—when we got clear of the small islands and out into the open loch we soon found that the water which had seemed so calm and still from the shore wasn't so calm and still: in fact there was quite a jabble; also, there was a quite perceptible breeze. But of course this latter was what we had been hoping for, so in short spells each pair pulled lustily at the oars to get at the earliest moment to the point where we could lie back and leave it to the breeze.

Just then a seemingly innocent wavelet broke on our bow and treated us to a surprisingly generous shower-bath. We moderated speed to lessen the risk of repetition, but despite every precaution every now and again we had another substantial splash. The churn had to be shifted—a delicate operation!—to let us get with the baler at the now considerable water in the bottom of the boat. Under such handicaps it took us nearer two hours than one to reach the longed-for point where we could up-sail; and then—would you believe it?—when, wet and weary, we did at last arrive at that point, there was the wind blowing, not from the east but from the nor'-nor'-east!—straight in our teeth from Rodil!

It was a bitter blow. Commonsense urged the wisdom of making back for Lochmaddy. Stubborn foolish pride prevented everybody from voicing it. Then after a few thought-packed moments:

"Not a hope of getting to Rodil to-night," firmly announced the skipper, "but the wind is going more to

3

the north, and by keeping close inshore we should have a little shelter and will try to make Hermetray of it for the night. If the wind goes down we may still get to Rodil in the morning in time for the Show."

Hermetray is one of the larger of the many small uninhabited islands to the south of the Sound of Harris. It was still a long three miles from where we were. The hoped-for shelter on the way to it was from the towering black rocks that form the coast northwards of the Weaver's Point. With an easterly breeze the back-surge from this bastion can be highly dangerous to small craft. In a gale the breakers there are stupendous. Our hope was that the wind would not go round to the east; and in that flimsily-founded hope we started pulling slowly and grimly for Hermetray.

Even now, as I write, the recollection of that desperately slow and dreary pull in a heavily laden cockle-shell below yon fearsome rocky ramparts makes me shudder. The shelter fell far short of what we had hoped: there was indeed a dangerous back-wash from the base of the cliffs, and but for the exciseman's superb handling of the little craft this story would certainly never have been written—by me or anybody else. If (as it happened) Willie Urquhart never took us from Lochmaddy to Rodil in his boat, in tribute to his memory and skill I am bound to record that on that awful afternoon he displayed twice as much of seamanship as would be required to do so on a moderately fine day.

The wind had increased ominously and I have a shrewd suspicion that for a while the amount of courage amongst us—always excepting the trusting lady and the intrepid skipper—wouldn't have amounted to as much as a half-pint. For my own part I know I was scared stiff. Yet I soon found that the quality of courage can be as infectious as that of fear: that courage is largely the fruit of faith in something or someone—including oneself. In this case, after our skipper had again and again saved us from being engulfed, it seemed that the seed of faith in him and his seamanship was planted in our minds; and as it grew and flourished, fear took a back seat and courage came to the front. Thus guided and encouraged, at long, long last we got to safety in the lee of Hermetray. Soon we would be ashore on that desolate island and would put into effect our plans for passing what was bound to be a rather uncomfortable night in the best open-air shelter we could find. Half the sandwiches were already well and truly eaten and only strict self-discipline had saved the other half. There was most of the bottle of whisky and half a dozen of beer. But if the storm continued and increased (as now seemed all too likely) it might be long enough before we got off the island. However, we were safe! and we would manage to subsist somehow for a few days.

.   .   .   .

In the main we were intent on looking for the best spot to make a landing on Hermetray, and it was more by good luck than presence of mind that some of us didn't fall overboard when Eoghan Beag yelled excitedly in Gaelic. "Look at this, boys! A vessel making for Lochmaddy!"

And sure enough there she was, a sturdy if rather rusty-looking craft, heading straight in for the loch. The possibility of relief came on us so suddenly that for a few moments we were dumbfounded. But soon the wits got going again. In half a minute we were in complete agreement: this must be the ship sent to take up the *Lapwing's* run. She would pick up the mails and stranded passengers, and be out and passing us again in less than an hour on her way to Rodil! We would pull back in the direction of Weaver's Point to be in a position to intercept her when she came out, get the Show party and paraphernalia hauled on board to be landed at Rodil, and leave Willie and Ewen to row themselves back in comparative safety to Lochmaddy. As simple as that! What a relief! How incredibly lucky!

So great was our delight at escaping the misery of perhaps three hungry days and nights on the island, we did not mind rowing back over the course we had so strenuously covered in the past two hours. Besides, it was much easier going with the wind, even if hoisting sail was out of the question. Soon we were half-way back to Weaver's Point and hoping every moment to have our surmise proved right by a reappearance of the relief ship. Nor had we long to wait for that!

" Pull like blazes, boys, to get right in her course and we will keep position there," came the order from the skipper. We obeyed so effectively that soon the ship was bearing straight down on us, and we were being yelled at in broadest Buchan by an angry man demanding to know what sort of bloody fools we thought we were, and adding some picturesque but quite unprintable opinions of his own on the subject. Also, to avoid running us down, the engines had been practically stopped.

" We want you to take us to Rodil," I yelled down wind.

" Rodil? " he bawled back. " Where's that? "

This came as a shock; but of course he could only be bluffing; so I countered, " Your first port of call in the south of Harris."

" Never there in my life, and am not going there now. I came to Lochmaddy to pick up a stranded shooting party and am to land them at Uig in Skye. And get out of there! " came angrily from the captain, who had now come to conduct the conversation.

This, coming from so authoritative a source, rather

punctured us. There was only one line left to us now, and we took it. We spoke portentously to the captain. We pleaded urgent business of State. The Secretary for Scotland would be a disappointed man if his highly placed officials should be unable to meet him at the Harris Agricultural Show because of the refusal of the captain of the *Moray View* to render them a courtesy that would cause a delay of less than an hour—and for which they were prepared to pay a reasonable fee. (May we be forgiven! The Secretary for Scotland wasn't going to the Harris Show that year, and we knew it. But, anyway, this turned out to be an occasion on which that distinguished Servant of the Crown proved really useful.)

After a brief consultation with his mate the captain protested, " But I don't know the course to Rodil, or the way in."

" Mr Rose," I bawled, " knows this coast from end to end and will take you safely there." As a matter of fact John knew the coast sufficiently well to do that on a clear day, even if he might not have passed muster with the Board of Trade.

Further consultation, then, " How much will you give? "

" How much do you want? "

" Five pounds."

" Right-o ! " yelled everyone in our boat in chorus.

Then the *Moray View* was manœuvred so as to allow us to get in on her sheltered side. Not till we started the job of transferring the boxes and ourselves to the ship did we fully realise its difficulties. One moment the wee boat would be away down near the keel of the ship and the next up so high that we were looking down at her deck. That half of our stuff—and of ourselves—didn't find a watery grave was a sort of miracle that must be largely attributed to the skill and strength of the men on the trawler, who were experts at snatching a box or a body at the right moment and holding on to haul it safely aboard.

In a surprisingly short time the desired amount of transfer was complete. Willie and Ewen backed out and headed their boat straight for the shelter that would be between the Weaver's Point and Lochmaddy pier. I passed over a cheque for five pounds, for which I got a duly stamped receipt in the name of David Main of the *Moray View*. Rose was put in charge of the ship and against a rousing nor'-easter directed her course to Rodil Bay, where we were safely transferred to the ferry boat and finally landed at the slip.

As we refreshed and warmed ourselves at the hospitable Rodil hotel that evening I'm not saying but there might have been a bit of being rather well pleased with ourselves. After all, you know—well, it did take a bit of doing !

Virtuously we retired at ten to be ready for the early start in the morning—and the Show.

.   .   .   .

Somewhere in the small hours we were wakened by the rattling of windows and various other indications of an uncommonly rough night. Nor was there another wink of sleep. With morning we got up, to realise that we were experiencing one of the great storms of the Hebrides. A howling, shrieking wind from the east that drove the waters of the Minch to break against the rocks and toss their spray two hundred feet higher than the headlands. A storm that continued all day and is still spoken of with awe. . . .

And there was *no* Show in Harris that year after all !

CHAPTER V

Orkney—A Rude Awakening

HAVING regard to its natural disadvantages of latitude, climate and severance from the mainland, it might be supposed that Orkney would be one of the most backward farming counties in Scotland; in fact, it is perhaps the most progressive and successful farming county in the whole of Britain. A stranger motoring there for the first time, on seeing a very fine lot of cattle in a roadside field, might well conclude that this must be a lot collected for competition at an agricultural show. But as he proceeds on his journey he becomes puzzled; for in the next field there is a similar lot of cattle—and in the next and the next! Gradually the truth dawns on him: they cannot *all* be going to a show! They are not: they are just Orkney's ordinary cattle.

Then he would notice that the whole countryside is peppered with poultry houses. Fifty years ago Orkney was at least as backward as its neighbours in this branch of farming. The first stimulus came from an Aberdonian who, with characteristic foresight, saw a fortune in Orkney's cheap eggs. This pioneer inaugurated systematic egg-collecting, first on the " mainland " and later throughout the islands. The eggs were promptly tested, graded and despatched to the markets at Leith and Aberdeen. Soon the reputation of Orkney eggs (hitherto rather unenviable) improved. They commanded a better price—which enabled the Aberdonian to pay a higher price to the producers, who were thus stimulated to greater and still greater production efforts. The number of poultry rapidly increased. Now a croft of no more than five acres may have on it up to a thousand hens; and not any old hens, but every bird well bred and carefully selected from healthy heavy-laying strains. Between the two big wars the annual value of Orkney's eggs was estimated at nearly £200,000. Now it has topped the half-million mark and is still rising.

In this matter of the general high standard of farming it may or may not be a significant fact that nearly two-thirds of the 3,250 agricultural holdings in Orkney are owned by their occupiers. How this came about is rather interesting. Soon after the termination of the 1914-18 war the Zetland family, to whom the greater part of Orkney belonged, decided to sell out. The first offer to sell in large lots did not attract a satisfactory response. The next move was to offer each holding to the sitting tenant at a reasonable price. This proved highly popular. Orcadians had prospered exceedingly during the war and were flush of cash. The great majority of them bought their holdings—and so became landlords! And a political cynic may find amusement in the reflection that, not many years after, for the first time in history, a hitherto stubbornly Liberal Orkney returned the Conservative candidate as their member of parliament!

Before the coming of the air service—that is, up till about fifteen years ago—the only way of getting to or from Orkney was by sea, and the shorter crossing was between Scrabster and Scapa. I read in the papers the other day that a new boat is being built to take the place of the *St. Ola*, which for over fifty years has been on that run. It is easy to imagine a vessel providing more luxurious accommodation than the old *Ola*, but it is mighty difficult to believe that anything tougher and safer than that little craft can be provided.

She wasn't by any means a new boat when I first crossed in her in 1902. The fact that she has never had any serious mishap in all these years and is still going strong, despite the marine hazards of two world wars and the turbulent tides and screaming storms of the Pentland Firth, is a remarkable tribute to those responsible for her and her passengers' safety. That first time I crossed was also the first time I had ever put to sea in a boat. I had heard so much about the Pentland Firth that I was prepared for an unpleasant experience. However, despite some considerable heaving and dipping at the bows (which in my ignorance I accepted as evidence of a rough crossing), neither on the outward nor homeward voyage did I feel the slightest sensation of sickness. As others of the family who had previously visited Orkney had returned with tales of the humiliating toll of the Firth, I was inclined to brag a bit and explain that sea-sickness was largely a result of apprehension. In fact, no one need be sea-sick who thought the right thoughts about the thing. Look at me! The suggestion that I must have had a good crossing was refuted by a reference to the heaving bows, and I was eager to show proof of my theory next time I crossed when, I hoped, it might be really *very* stormy. Well, next October I was Orkney-bound again. When the train arrived at Georgemas Junction (where normally passengers for Orkney take the branch line to Thurso and thence bus for the boat at Scrabster) there was the platform porter bawling: " Passengers for the *Ola* carry on to Wick."

When that happens it means that the weather is so wild that the *Ola* can't make Scrabster and has to run to Wick instead. Good! It was to be a really rough crossing. I would have a chance of proving my theory!

In less than an hour we were in Wick, where we found the few people in the streets chasing hats and dodging slates and chimney-cans that rioted through the town. With difficulty we got to the quay where the *Ola* was berthed.

At that time she was commanded by Captain Robertson, a spare, white-whiskered, keen-eyed man with a local reputation as an intrepid seaman whose place it would be hard, if not impossible, to fill. But when the time for that came the owners were fortunate in that they had ready to hand one who in every respect was soon to prove a worthy successor—the late much loved and lamented Captain Swanson, who was then a young fair-haired, blue-eyed Scandinavian whose great seamanship was matched by his unfailing courtesy and his gift for friendship.

This day at Wick, no doubt after much anxious reckoning of risks, old Captain Robertson finally decided to sail. Of sixteen intending passengers, nine decided not to go. Only seven—four never-say-die "commercials," one elderly woman going home to Orkney, one very portly gent going north for some rough shooting and my indomitable self—were prepared to risk it. In a matter of minutes the ropes were let go and we were under way.

The lady passenger proved an immediate casualty; as soon as she came on board she turned a pale green colour of countenance and crept to oblivion down below. The corpulent sporting gentleman and two of the commercials also quickly disappeared. The other two and myself manfully paced what small strip of deck there is and inhaled the stimulating salt sea breeze.

Going up the Caithness coast we were in comparative shelter, although, after my previous experience, this seemed to me a very stormy day indeed. But there was that grand feeling of physical well-being and the subtle joy that comes from demonstrating a theory. Then all of a sudden one of my companions appeared to lose interest in our conversation, gurgled a throaty " 'scuse me ! " and dived for a companion-way.

" What's wrong? " I asked.

" Poor Davie! He's signed off! " the remaining commercial explained.

" Dear me! Very strange! " said I.

" Oh well, of course, it's not too good even here," my companion expounded, " but believe me it's a mill pond to what it will be when we round Duncansby Head and get into the Firth! " Then he added, " And as that will be in the next few minutes I'm going while the going is good." So there I was, the proud sole survivor on deck! Just then the mate came along and suggested I should go below as soon it might be " a bit dirty."

" Oh, thanks " I said, " but that is what I want. This is grand! "—as the bows rose higher and plunged lower than before. The ship also began doing other queer delightful things ; squirming side-ways like a crab ; heeling over this way and that, plunging and bucking violently. While I was enjoying all this, and mid-way in a deep inspiration of ozone, there came over the side with startling suddenness a monstrous mass of solid sea that just didn't sweep me overboard. But it did lay me prostrate against the rails and drenched me to the skin—and it wasn't warm! I had also, involuntarily, swallowed a salty pint. With more of hurt pride than apprehension I clutched at the rails and pulled myself to my feet.

" Get down below. We don't want you to get washed overboard," commanded the mate.

It was only when I started to descend the steps to the saloon that there came to me the first premonition of the possibility of the theory breaking down. Nor was I left long in doubt; in seconds there was within me a complete transition from the jolly outlook to hitherto uncharted depths of physical and mental misery as the first moiety of tollage cascaded down the stair and a violent lurch of the ship pitched me after it.

Sitting at the bottom of the steps in what had so

recently formed part of my personal content, I made
desperate efforts to anticipate the direction of the next
lurch so that I might reach in safety a vacant part of the
cushioned bench which surrounded the saloon. But
always I guessed wrong: the next move of the ship was
quite unpredictable and my every attempt at reaching
the desired spot violently frustrated.

My objective was the vacant space between where one
of the commercials and the sporting gentleman lay
stretched and strapped to the bench. Fatty, on the near
side of the vacancy, lay on the broad of his back, and
sound asleep. By now I had arrived at the fireplace in
the middle of the saloon and was grimly hugging the
stove-pipe, waiting the chance of one last dive to where
I longed to lie. Just for a moment the ship steadied,
and I sprang for it! But alas! who can foretell the
puckish ploys of a plunging ship? Anyway, just as I
jumped, the *Ola* did something which lifted me clean off
my feet; instead of plunking down where I meant to,
my stern, with all my considerable weight on top of it,
came plunk down on the highest round of Fatty's tummy!
One can hardly conceive of a ruder awakening, and
certainly his yell did justice to the occasion. In his wild
physical reaction, too, the strap which bound him to the
bench broke, and the next heave of the ship had us both
sprawling and slithering helplessly over the floor of the
saloon.

But hold! enough of a pitiful tale and an exploded
theory. In forty-six years I have crossed the Pentland
Firth in a boat one hundred and twenty times; occasionally—very occasionally—in comparative calm and comfort.
But, weather fierce or fine, it's a grand country to visit,
and the courtesy and friendliness of officers and men of
the *Ola* unfailing.

CHAPTER VI

Locked Out—Fire Brigade—Phantom Funeral—William
Wallace from Australia

FROM infancy I was brought up in an atmosphere of
hot hostility to, and contempt for, landed estate factors.
Such we regarded as the natural enemies of crofters;
much more so than the lairds! Tales of their tyranny
and turpitude were in prime favour at the ceilidh, and
many were the stories of that kind that I listened to in
the long winter evenings as we sat in semi-circle round
the blazing peat.

That there was solid foundation for some of these tales
was undoubtedly true. It appears that, until towards
the end of the nineteenth century, many Highland lairds
and factors alike—just as in the case of manufacturers
and their factory hands—failed to grasp the vital fact
that their own and their tenants' interests were identical:
that a régime of rack-renting and harsh treatment—
which discouraged improvement of land and buildings
and engendered hatred—must in the long run inevitably
react detrimentally on the laird himself as well as on
his crofter tenant. Doubtless, even in these bad old days,
there would be a proportion of decent lairds and factors
who were far-seeing and humane in their dealings with
their smaller tenants, but he would be an unpopular
member of the ceilidh circle that made mention of such!
Reared in that creed it can be readily believed that
when my official duties first brought me in direct and
frequent contact with estate factors I was prepared to see
an ogre in every one.

Here and there, indeed, I did come across the genuine
monster, but after many years I am happy publicly to
avow that of the scores of estate factors I have had dealings
with—and not infrequently hotly contested dealings—the

term " gentleman " would apply to the great majority; the
ogre is the exception. And I am also happy to think that
in most cases (while the ceilidh circle may be reluctant
to abandon their century-old right—and duty—of
anathematising the arch enemy!) crofters now know in
their inner hearts that their factor is quite a decent,
kindly man, and that in any ceilidh censure of him they
are merely chanting the refrain of an old song that has
lost its sting and meaning.

Personally, I have been privileged to enjoy the hospitality and friendship of crofter and factor alike in every
part of the Highlands and Islands, and have not hesitated
to take full advantage of that circumstance to promote
their mutual interests. With that in view I usually make
a point of calling to pay my respects at the local factor's
house or office. One day in Skye, rather late in the
evening, I went over to the factor's house for a chat and
to get the low-down on Skye affairs generally—in regard
to which, for one who seldom goes far from Portree, he
is amazingly well-informed.

As was not unusual on such occasions, " the time flew
by with tentless heed " and we were surprised to see the
clock creeping to 1 A.M. I had said nothing at the hotel
about the possibility of being late; it would be awkward
if in ignorance of my absence they had locked up and
gone to bed. The assistant factor, who was with us and
lodged down in the village, hurried off with me. It was
bright moonlight without a breath of wind. Not a
creature—bar a prowling cat—did we see as we hurried
to the hotel—to find its massive door well and truly
locked! With guilty conscience I pulled the bell. It
clanged like a fire alarm. Goodness gracious! that
would waken everyone in the house! The assistant factor
stood by and we waited for deserved reproach. But
minutes passed and nobody came. The assistant factor

suggested I should go with him to his digs and sleep on a sofa. That was very kind—but dash it all surely that bell should waken someone! I gave it another tug—which caused it to set up a frightful clangour sufficient to waken all but the dead. Another shrinking wait. Not a sound of anybody moving.

We went to have a look at the windows. Every one on the ground floor was securely shut. There was one on the first floor slightly open. That was the window of a private sitting-room which was converted into a bedroom only occasionally under pressure of demand. The hotel was now fairly full, but this private sitting-room had not been commandeered; at least it had not been earlier that evening as I happened to know.

If only I could reach that window our problem was solved. But it was twelve feet up, and all attempts at scaling the wall proved futile. Then the assistant factor remembered about the Fire Brigade ladder. This ladder was kept in a long shed up near The Knock. In the gable of the shed there was a hole through which, in case of emergency, it could be pulled out for action.

So off we set to investigate on the spot. There was the shed right enough, but there was a rank growth of nettles obscuring the hole. These we trampled down sufficiently to allow of one getting a grip of the butt end of the ladder to pull it out. Not a move! Presumably there had been no call on its service since it and the shed had been put there some twenty years earlier. Only one pair of hands could get a proper grip of the ladder, so for our next effort the assistant factor took that grip and I gripped him round the waist.

One—two—heave! . . . and the ladder came away so suddenly that we were both laid flat among the nettles . . . nor were we long in getting to our feet! Then more cautiously we proceeded to extract it through the hole, my companion standing close to the shed and I at the outer end going farther and farther away with every pull, until we began to wonder how that shed could possibly contain so long a thing.

We had soon noticed that what we were extracting was really a sort of Siamese Twins arrangement of two ladders firmly lashed together. At long last the extraction was complete: the Twins were lying among the nettles. We untied the lashing to free them and then—the assistant factor near the front end and I at the rear—with ladder hoisted on shoulders we marched in step towards the hotel.

On arrival below the open window it was soon all too evident that our ladder was much too long for our modest purpose. Set at a safe angle for climbing, it reached up to beyond the second-floor windows and at that slope did not come within six feet of the wall passing the window we wanted to get to.

On the other hand, when we set the top of the ladder against the sill of our window, the bottom of it was far away out in the roadway and the slope so flat that it seemed very doubtful if it would carry my rather substantial weight. But there was no alternative : we must test it. Cautiously I began to go forward step by step. When I had got to nearly half the length of the ladder, but still a long way from the window, there was an ominous down-sway followed by a loud crack ! I jumped to the ground just in time to save the ladder from a complete break in two ! And that was that; so we shouldered the confounded thing again, marched it back to The Knock and left it to lie in the nettles with its futile fellow.

It was now after two o'clock in the morning and we made straight for my friend's lodging—which happened to be the house of a local tradesman and away on the other side of the hotel. As we were about to enter at the door what should we see lying against the garden wall but a twelve-foot ladder! Well, I'm blest! The very thing we had been looking for! So (in the same order) we shouldered this one and marched off down towards the hotel.

But now the moon had retired behind a mass of black cloud and there was an eerie gloom over the village. As we were passing along the main street what should we dimly discern coming up the steep harbour brae but the form of a notorious village worthy who had had a riotous night, and was now making heavy weather of it coming up that hill. But gamely he rose to his feet again prepared to carry on. The top of the brae could not be far away? With somewhat bleared vision he tried to gauge the extent of effort still required to reach level ground. It was then we heard his moan of horror as, miraculously sobered on the instant, he fled down the hill again as if pursued by Evil Spirits—a conviction in which he was doubtless confirmed by the howls of our laughter which pierced the stillness of the night. Later we learned that for months the poor man went about sober and in daily dread of the death of which he had had so dreadful a prevision that night at the top of the pier brae. For, out of our marching along with the ladder in the gloom of the night, what easier for a scared and imaginative Celt than to construct a phantom funeral procession?

As we had guessed, the ladder proved just right for our purpose. Up I scrambled and pushed the window up another foot to allow of an easy entry. By now there was no light from the moon, so that the room was in darkness. I did listen for any sound from within just in case it might be occupied; not a sound! But of course the noise I had already made pushing up the window couldn't have failed to waken anyone there might be! So I gave the O.K. and a good-night to the assistant factor, who marched off home with the ladder on his shoulder.

I knew that the door of the room opened on to the

corridor, not immediately opposite the window, but away at the far corner. In order to avoid a collision in the dark with a table which usually stood in the middle of the room, I decided to feel my way along the west wall and then the south wall to the door. Now, as a test of the power of observation, I cannot think of anything stiffer than trying to steer a noiseless way in the dark through a room with whose every item of furniture you may consider yourself to be familiar. As I groped along in the dark my feet and my face came in violent contact with quite unexpected objects. The coal scuttle did not seem to be in its usual place ; on the wall, pictures and crockery arrested my hands in most unexpected places, and with alarmingly noiseful results. Then, when half way along the south wall and not far from the much-desired door, my heart misfired several times before starting to race at high speed. The cause was the faint but unmistakable sound of a human snore ! I stood stock still—there it was again ! Peering back against the modicum of light coming from the window I could dimly trace the outline of a bed with a hump showing beneath its counterpane. No head or any other part of a human being could I make out; but there was the bed—and there indubitably was the hump ; and the hump rose and fell rhythmically with the gentle snore. Perspiration oozed from every pore. Good heavens ! Was it a male or a female snore? But how could man or woman sleep through all yon din? If a man, and he suddenly wakened up, he would be justified in doing bodily hurt to the now boneless intruder ! If a woman she would probably scream and perhaps incur permanent injury to her reason !

This was clearly a place where it would be good for me not to be. Cautiously I edged in what I judged to be the direction of the door. Mercifully I encountered no clattering impediment. Soon the knob was in my hand. Gently I turned it, stepped softly into the corridor and pulled the door shut. At that moment I thought I heard a voice say " Eh! What! Who's there? " But perhaps it was just imagination? Softly I crept to the electric switch at the stairhead and got light to see the way to my room. It was quite a while before I could compose myself and go to sleep.

At eight o'clock Katie came in with a cup of tea. " Och," says she, " so you got in all right! I was off duty last night and forgot to tell the mistress to make sure you would be in before she locked the door and I was afraid you might be locked out! "

" Katie," I said, " was it a man or a woman who was in No. 4 last night? "

" A man—a man of the name of William Wallace, from Australia. Why? "

" Do you know if he is alive—or dead? "

" Dead! No indeed! He went off with the boat this morning."

" Was he quite all right? "

" Yes! He was quite all right as far as I could see; but he was asking me if there was a ghost in the house. He thought he heard one going about in the night! "

" Listen, Katie . . .," and as I proceeded with a brief outline of the night's happenings Katie's mirth mounted to hysteria. " Stop you," says she, " till I tell the mistress! "

And so, should any of the Portree police force of that day still survive and happen to read this, they will at last have the solution of the " ladders-in-the-nettles " problem that puzzled them for so long. And should William Wallace from Australia by a more remote chance see it, he will have the explanation of his ghost-disturbed sleep. But it would be too much to hope that he can still sleep as soundly o' nights as he did as a young man in Portree so many years ago.

CHAPTER VII

Crossing the Fords

ONE day we travelled from Lochboisdale to Lochmaddy. The distance is only a matter of forty-two miles, but in that are included the two famous fords of the Hebrides— the South Ford of about a mile, between the islands of South Uist and Benbecula, and the North Ford of fully four miles, between Benbecula and North Uist. Now a beautiful bridge spans the former, and hopes are high in the Islands that before long they will see a similar bridge over the North Ford. When that happens even the presently diminished travelling time between the two capitals of the Uists will be further diminished; then, without moving out of your comfortable seat in a car, you can do it in a matter of an hour! Well, well! and there was yon time we went " over the fords " on a day some thirty-five years ago.

Of course we had it carefully planned out in the hotel the night before, timing all our movements to synchronise with the immutable laws of the tides.

" With this wind from the west you cannot depend on much time between the opening to the closing of the fords," declared the genial old autocrat of the hotel, whose dictum on such a point no sane traveller dared dispute; " you can get the first of the South Ford at Carnan at eleven o'clock and you must be over the North Ford and at Carnish not later than half-past two. That means that the wagonette will leave here in the morning at eight o'clock prompt. You will be at Carnan before eleven. MacLean will put you over in his cart to Crea-gorry where you can get a bite of food. The Creagorry wagonette should be at Gramisdal not later than half past one to give the Carnish trap a chance of getting you over in time. If the Lochmaddy brake is waiting for you at Carnish at three, you should be at the end of your journey by five o'clock at latest."

Splendid! and so it was arranged. Various telegrams were despatched in the hope of ensuring the necessary transport.

With a bit of luck here and there the journey sometimes did actually work out that way in those days. But the crossing of the fords was always an adventure, subject to the qualification which we usually referred to as " D.V. and W.P."—and this day the gods and the weather were in all-out opposition.

How fortunate that often the morning gives little indication of the troubles that the day may bring! We left with spirits in keeping with the wine in the air and the beautiful high-stepping pair of greys. Past Daliburgh (where in this land of leisure not a smoke yet showed) and on by Askernish, Bornish, Howmore and Crogarry with their spacious machairs stretching out to infinity in the west and their hundreds of highland cattle; over the causeway that straddles Loch Bee (that rendezvous of the white swan and Princess of fishing lochs!), and, well on schedule, pulled up at Carnan—where the greys were to eat and refresh preparatory to taking a party from Crogarry to Lochboisdale later in the day.

But now we had our first spot of trouble. One of the Carnan carts had gone over on the night ford and had waited in Creagorry to take another party back at mid-day. Following on receipt of our telegram the lad had gone to the hill to search for the other Carnan horse, which had just come in with a cracked hoof and a broken shoe—which condition could be remedied only when the smith could be retrieved from where he had gone to work at peats nearly two miles away. The lad was now away for the smith—who did turn up half an hour later and wasn't long at his job; but as we entered the South Ford we were already an hour behind schedule. The ford near the north shore was none too good, but we managed to splash through with the horses' feet still finding bottom.

At Creagorry came a real shock: a telegram from Carnish saying all conveyances otherwise engaged and advising us to take the Creagorry wagonette right on to Carnish.

Our friend at Creagorry was not for this plan at all. For one thing the sun had gone to hide behind banks of black clouds that had gathered up and now raced overhead; and then, if he did put us to Carnish he would certainly not get back home by the same ford—which would mean either his staying at Carnish till afternoon tomorrow or returning by the ford in the middle of the night. But these men of " The Fords " never let travellers down if they can possibly avoid that; so at the back of one o'clock we started off in the Creagorry wagonette with its two tough ponies that knew too well what was in front of them to make any show-off other than flattened ears, indicating a determination to get on with the job.

The North Ford is really a double one: there is one water channel near the Benbecula shore and another near the North Uist side. In the most favourable of crossings there will be anything up to three feet of water in these channels. After negotiating the first, for nearly a mile you are on dead flat firm sand (if you are careful to keep to the course marked by a row of wrack-covered boulders!) till you reach the notorious Caigean Rocks through which, over the vilest of tracks, horses, harness and carriage twist and groan and creak most alarmingly. After this liver-stirring in the Caigean there is another stretch of firm sand till you come to the Carnish channel— and the feature of this ford is its inconstancy! here this tide, there the next, and goodness knows where it may be safe to chance it another time. At one hitherto " safe " place, a tide of the week before had scooped out a hole eight feet deep into which Donald Archie's good horse stepped, dog-cart and all. That was the end of a gallant beast, and it was only by the grace of God that it wasn't the end of Donald Archie too.

This day when we came in sight of the water in the Gramisdal ford even Angus the driver was taken aback. Instead of twenty yards wide or so it was nearer a hundred yards, and the water was dark and ruffled ! Bad—very bad looking ! Was the tide still receding or was it already on the turn?

The horses stopped. Angus got down and with his boot streaked the sand parallel to the water's edge. Anxiously we waited to note the result. The mark in the sand filled with water.

" She's on the turn already. I don't like the look of it," pronounced Angus. " Even if we get through here we will have to race for it to get over the Carnish ford."

There was some talk of discretion being the better part. Angus made another mark in the sand—from a study of which he seemed to gather some slender hope.

" Take your bags on your knees and keep a good grip; we'll try it," came the commander's decision.

Pluckily into the dark water stepped the ponies. Down—down—to knees !—to bellies !—to ribs ! Up rushed the water into the box of the wagonette; up went our feet to escape the flood. Only the horses' backs were now above water. In a moment they were down to it and swimming strongly. The wagonette swung round in the current, but the ponies with only a few quiet words of encouragement from Angus held gamely on. Soon they got bottom again and clambered out to the other side.

" Good boys ! " said Angus, patting the pair, " just a minute to get your wind." And then we were off at full gallop for the Caigean.

While winding through the Caigean what should we meet but another of the Creagorry drivers leading a horse and carrying a bundle of gig cushions.

" What's wrong with you, Donald? " inquired Angus.

" Went into a new hole in the Carnish ford and snapped the axle," Donald explained. " I'm putting the cushions above high water, and then I'll have to ride like the devil for Gramisdal and swim for it. But where on earth do you think you are going to? You'll never make the Carnish ford of it with the water like yon."

" And I cannot get back to Gramisdal in time: the horses haven't the breath left in them for it," said Angus quietly after a moment's reflection. " Where exactly is the hole? "

" It is right on the track that we were using yesterday— but for heaven's sake watch yourselves ! I must be off ; " and Donald astride the black horse made off like the wind for Gramisdal. Quite right, too : by waiting he could do no good and would but add to the list of possible casualties.

We set off for our own problem—and I cannot recollect the slightest effort on the part of any of us to get a joke out of the situation.

One glance at the state of the Carnish ford was enough to appal anyone. Here was no narrow channel of water with firm sand bottom, but a wide expanse of surging sea which blotted out all the usual landmarks and guide-stones.

" Not too good at all," was Angus's masterly under-statement of the situation.

We got a glimpse of Donald's dog-cart floating past a rock on the now fast-flowing tide. All trace of its wheel-marks had vanished. Angus did his best to decide where yesterday's line of ford had been and drove the pair into the water on a line calculated to clear us of the danger. That was the most fearsome drive I have ever had. The bottom was fiendishly uneven. One moment the horses would be swimming; the next they would be stumbling on submerged banks of sand—while all the time the distance to the other side seemed to be increasing instead of lessening. We were too concerned to keep our backsides out of the water to bother about our soaking cases. Out of the black sky came a real snorting shower of sleet. It was in the middle of that that the near-horse almost all but disappeared, while the off, in comparatively shallow water, struggled desperately to keep clear of the hole which had swallowed his companion. There was some confusion of pulling and drawing to no purpose; the traces got ravelled. The near-horse was being held under by the pole. Angus threw aside the now useless reins, scrambled on to the back of the off-horse and with a small hatchet and strong knife contrived to cut traces, etc., so as to give both horses their freedom. Immediately the horses made back for the safety of the Caigean; nor were we long in following their example.

But for the substantial flask which one of us happened to have in his pocket there might have been serious consequences to our wretched stranding on these dreary rocks for four hours—till a boat from Carnish came to take us off and to retrieve what we could of our sodden cases. It was after seven when we got to the little window and the big peat fire at Carnish—where the Lochmaddy conveyance had been waiting since three o'clock; and between one delay and another—largely taking appropriate " precautions " against pneumonia—it wasn't far off midnight when we pulled up at Lochmaddy hotel.

Usually there is a streak of consolation in the most adverse of circumstances. One of the party on that memorable crossing was one of my big shots from Edinburgh to whom I had been telling some tales of the Fords and who, having crossed them for the first time only two days before under perfect conditions of white sand and sunny skies, had left me in no doubt as to his opinion of my veracity!

CHAPTER VIII

Court of the Dogs—Many Clients—Keeping the Peace—
The Shah

In regard to the keeping of dogs, farmers and shepherds in this country are in a favoured position: provided the dog is kept for the purpose of tending sheep or cattle, no licence fee is payable in respect of it.

Up till about forty years ago such exemptions were granted rather promiscuously. Each year the Inland Revenue people sent to every farmer and shepherd a printed form setting forth that the dog (or dogs) was kept solely for the purpose of tending sheep or cattle. This statement was signed by the owner, and without further ado official exemption from tax payment was granted.

Very likely there would be a smattering of such exemptions held on very thin grounds! Certainly, in some parts of the Highlands there was an inordinate number of dogs which—not being strenuously engaged in the vocation in respect of which their master benefited in the matter of taxation—found their highest joy in life in chasing motor cars, and thereby proving a perfect menace to drivers in the early days of motoring. The first hoot of a motor was the signal for every dog in the township—and what swarms there were of them!—setting off hell-for-leather for the roadside to attack this monstrous thing that had come to disturb the peace of the countryside. They would yap and bark furiously at the front wheels, and seemed never to understand why the monster did not, like a sheep or a cow or a horse, turn tail and flee instead of carrying straight on. Some of them would follow for a mile, keeping up their puzzled but futile yapping at the thing that would neither stop nor turn. Then, what was left of them would go back to their homes, with tails erect, consciously proud of having done their best; and in no way dismayed or discouraged at the sound of the next motor horn.

You will notice I have said "what was left of them." That is because sometimes the casualty list was heavy. I remember one occasion when my driver bagged seven dogs in less than four miles. Another day he had a record bag of nine in the one run. I was not his passenger on this occasion, but in subsequent Court proceedings the sheriff, instead of imposing a fine, complimented the driver on his valuable service to the public. It appeared that his Honour had himself experienced considerable inconvenience and annoyance from the alert and vociferous dogs of the district. Nor am I as callous in this matter as may seem. To me, as to every decent motor driver, the avertable killing of a dog is a most reprehensible and distressing occurrence. But in those days very few of the owners made any effort at controlling their dogs: the latter were allowed to chase motors to their heart's content. It was mostly the really wily ones that ran to the roadside well ahead of the car and lay concealed in a side-drain to make a surprise all-out spring at the front wheels when they came along that got run over. With such, no driver had a ghost of a chance of steering clear.

It was probably as a result of this trouble with the dogs that there was then introduced a more discriminating régime in the matter of granting exemptions from tax. It was now open to any responsible citizen to lodge with the authorities an objection to the granting of exemption in any specified case or cases; and following on such objection no exemption was granted unless the dog-owner proved before the sheriff that he was legally entitled to it.

Throughout the Hebrides such objections were lodged

in hundreds; and the perturbation and anger which this further threat to their rights and privileges caused amongst the island crofters—every one of whom regards his dog with utmost pride and affection—will be readily appreciated. Not even the crime of murder could have created wider concern and indignation. In every ceilidh house from Loch Seaforth to Barra Head the threat of being rendered dogless—for so the refusal of exemption seemed to be generally interpreted—was the one and only topic. For it was in this area that all the landlords (advised, it was alleged, by the " Factor Dubh " of vivid memory, who was also a lawyer) had acted as one, and lodged objection to every dog-tax exemption on their estates. This involved 1,542 dog-owners and 1,679 dogs. To what extent the Factor Dubh was in fact responsible for initiating the campaign can never now be ascertained, but there is no doubt in my mind that it would be difficult to find a pair with a stronger sense of puckish humour, or more ably equipped for such a ploy, than himself and his friend and legal opposite number Alasdair " Iain " (MacDonald)—who, as I write, is still going strong. Be that as it may, the gauntlet was now in the ring: the battle was joined. The Factor Dubh—hitherto champion of the crofters in their Land Law " Reform " battles—was now acting for the landlords! Alasdair— then a young and ardent antagonist—acted for all of the 1,542 dog-owners.

The case was put down for hearing at Lochmaddy on a Wednesday at 10 A.M. The great majority of the owners determined to appear in person to promote the cause of justice so far as was possible in a wicked world. Other members of the family came in support. Wednesday's boat would be too late for the people from Barra, and as there was no north-going boat on the Tuesday, they travelled by the Monday's boat. There was a strong representation from Harris on Tuesday, many crossing the Sound in sail-boats. On Tuesday morning, too, the trek from the south end of South Uist started and gathered strength as it went north over "The Fords." Finally people from all over North Uist came in on the Wednesday morning. The resulting crowd was the biggest ever seen at Lochmaddy and is likely to hold that distinction for a long time to come.

In anticipation of so large a gathering the Chief Constable had arranged that there should be at Lochmaddy for two days a full muster of the Islands' police force. Presumably the underlying idea was to ensure the maintenance of order. Anyhow, it didn't quite work out that way. Actually, while there was a good deal of dramming and some candid expression of opinion in regard to the intelligence of "them that wass at the bottom of all this troupple," there was nothing approaching a disturbance of the peace; with the result that seven genial policemen found themselves staying in an hotel and with very little to do: a positive gift, as one might say, for the old gentleman whose proverbial concern is to provide mischief for idle hands.

They were good fellows and friendly towards humanity, and so many people wanted to offer them good fellowship and hospitality. Besides, there was considerable conviviality amongst themselves. Moreover—and most unfortunate of all—they made the Highlander's usual mistake on such occasions: the mistake of depending entirely on liquid refreshment and scorning to eat solid food. So it was that in more than one instance the respective rôles of police and public were reversed. In particular one member of the force gave considerable concern to four of us who had got away from the general turmoil to the smoke-room and were enjoying a quiet game of solo. Somehow this policeman had got it into his head that we were far gone in drink and that it was his duty to stand by and see us safely to bed; a complete inversion of the facts. So he lay down on a sofa on the broad of his back to be ready to do the needful by us when the game finished. But there was a " kitty on," and as is the way with kitties, it took a long time to clear. When at long last the game ended, our guardian angel was sound asleep. Nay, more: he was dead to the world ! We shook him. We gripped his nose. We rubbed his ears. We put cold water down his neck. He snored on. The idea of carrying sixteen stone of inert humanity up a twisted stair was pondered, but dismissed as impracticable. He must be wakened up and induced to contribute some measure of self-transport.

It was the exciseman who had the brain-wave. A cherished pet of the lady of the hotel at that time was an out-size half-bred Persian cat; an affectionate creature delighting in more warmth than was always available in the wind-swept Hebrides. Its favourite couch was a chair-cushion which its mistress had warmed at the fire. On that it would squat and purr and purr in a physical ecstasy. Soon there would come the peak-period of bliss when some obscure feline instinct caused it to dig its claws into the cushion at every purring intake; a habit which, when indulged on human knees instead of a cushion, had often caused yells of anguish and some profane language. For this poor cat the stir caused in the hotel by *Cuirt nan con* was sheer nightmare: every room and corner of the place crowded with noisy human beings occupying not merely its favourite chair but all the other chairs as well—and even the steps in the stairs ! A dozen times that day we had heard the anguished yell of " the Shah " when coarse tackety boots came crashing down on his tender toes. Thus battered and kicked from pillar to post, with that extra instinct cats have for ensuring their own comfort, the Shah had at last found his way into the comparative quiet of the smoke-room and was doing his best to retrieve his dignity on a corner of the hearth-rug while we went on with our game. But the fire was getting low. By the time we cleared off the kitty the last bit of peat was reduced to ashes, and the poor Shah was faced by the horror of a cold and comfortless night. Imagine, therefore, his surprise and joy at finding himself being lifted by gentle hands and placed on a cushion warmer and more delectable than he had ever known! It was the bare, expansive lower abdomen of the arm of the law, which we had discreetly but adequately exposed as a cushion for the distracted Shah. Expert that he was, it did not take that intelligent animal long to realise that he was on to a good thing. Down he squatted, " purr, purr, purr," in rapid crescendo, while we stood clear for action. Nor did we have long to wait. Within a minute the Shah's eyes were closed in a delirium of delight. Soon the big bramble-bush claws would . . . " Baaaa! Oooich! " . . . And on the instant there was the widest-awake policeman imaginable; nor was he ever clear as to the cause of his rude awakening, for we assumed an air of utmost innocence, while the Shah, scared at the astounding reaction to his loving embrace, had vanished out of the door as if scalded by boiling water.

On the Wednesday morning nearly every one of fifteen hundred and forty clients was anxious to have a personal interview with Alasdair Iain before the Court would open. There were, of course, many of them who were strangers to him, and as he and I had neighbouring offices in the old Temperance Hotel building there was a good deal of confusion in regard to names. Dozens pushed their way into my room, each anxious that his man-of-business might understand his case at first hand; and even when I managed to explain that I wasn't the right

MacDonald for his purpose I still had to hear the rest of the story—partly perhaps, because there wasn't a hope of getting near Alasdair anyway. Soon the demand for him was so overwhelming that Alasdair decided he must go out to the road and give a short open-air address. The crowd extended along the road nearly from the hotel to the bank. A table was carried out and placed in position. Alasdair mounted the rostrum. His intention was to give them a short résumé of the points in the case. It proved to be, surely, the shortest speech on record, and I am terribly sorry that the story of it is so utterly incapable of adequate translation that I am not attempting any and must leave it in the original for the more fortunate readers to savour. Below is all that was said—and the merriment evoked in a crowd so appreciative of humour was such as to effectively kill any further attempt at serious talk. None appreciated the humour more keenly than Alasdair, who, shrewd psychologist that he is, and having got his audience in the best of spirits, warmly complimented the old man on his shaft of wit and assured all that he would do his utmost on their behalf.

ALASDAIR (in yon firm impressive voice of his). " A'Chairdean! Mudheighinn Cuirt nan con tha'n so. . . . "

BEARDED BODACH FROM BARRA (slowly, distinctly and with hearty emphasis). " Mata! B'e sin Cuirt nan galla! "

.   .   .   .

The Court room had normal seating for about a hundred people. This morning it had three times that number packed into it. The bulk of the crowd had to content themselves on the landings and stairs and out on the front green.

After some preliminary sparring by the lawyers the Factor Dubh outlined his case briefly and brightly as was his wont. In his view there had been gross laxity in the granting of exemptions. There were ten dogs on the Islands for every one required for the purposes which earned exemption in terms of the Act. These dogs were a menace to sheep and cattle, and a public nuisance. He would argue before his Lordship that the vast majority of dog-owners in the Islands, being merely crofters, could not qualify for tax-exemption as *farmers* at all—and he would ask for judgment accordingly.

But Alasdair Iain has had a busy over-night session fortifying himself against just such an attack. He has studied carefully the wording of the Act. He has also consulted an agricultural dictionary and the relevant sections of a ponderous and newly published encyclopædia of agriculture—all of which authoritative tomes he respectfully placed at the disposal of his Lordship (and some of which I did not recover for a very long time!).

His case was quite clear and logical:

A. Every farmer who keeps a dog (or dogs) for tending sheep or cattle is entitled to exemption from payment of tax.

B. There is no essential difference between " farmer " and " crofter " in regard to the right to exemption. Essentially and legally all crofters must be regarded as farmers so far as the right to exemption is concerned.

C. Therefore, all his clients who are crofters are entitled to exemption, not necessarily in respect of one dog only. The Act says " dog or dogs." It also says " sheep *or* cattle " (either of which, Alasdair conceded, must be read in the plural—but in a minimum of two!)

" And so, m'lord," Alasdair concluded, " my submission is that such of my clients as are crofters—and the great majority are—are, *ipso facto*, farmers, and every one of them, if he keeps on his place even no more than two sheep *or* two cattle is entitled to exemption from tax in respect of a dog *or* dogs for tending such sheep or cattle."

His Lordship was so impressed by this logic and argument and the authoritative tomes that the case—which we expected might not finish that day—was over in half an hour, with a verdict in favour of the crofters. Only a few dog-owners who, for one reason or another, fell short of the legal status of crofter were refused exemption. Well over fourteen hundred duly qualified. It was a great victory for them and for their lawyer. Moreover, as the latter was awarded expenses against the objecting parties in respect of each of his clients, there was just cause for a little celebration amongst us at the hotel that night.

CHAPTER IX

Agricultural Confusion—American Beef—Training in Diplomacy

ON my appointment as a member of the Scottish Land Court quite a number of people phoned my wife to say they were delighted, etc.—but what exactly *was* this Scottish Land Court? What did it or they *do*? The poor woman did her best to explain, but soon even she found herself rather tied up in knots about the respective functions of it and its several related bodies. Although not insensible of the common human aptitude to take less intelligent interest in the work of others than in one's own, I confess to a little wounded dignity at such widespread ignorance of the functions of the august body that was now to have the inestimable advantage of my wisdom. Frankly, though, it is perhaps not surprising that, even in the minds of normally intelligent people, there should be some ambiguity; for, in addition to the Scottish Land Court have we not also got a Department of Agriculture for Scotland, Agricultural Colleges, Agricultural Executive Committees and the S.A.O.S. (Scottish Agricultural Organisation Society)? Indeed we have, and a Farmers' Union and a Farm-Servants' Union, and the great Highland and Agricultural Society besides innumerable lesser Unions, Associations and Breed Societies; all charged with some statutory duty or corporate responsibility in connection with the good of the land and of the people living on it—and therefore, of course, of the good of the country as a whole. So perhaps it is not surprising that, in trying to grasp the exact nature and functions of so many bodies, some people " lose the place."

A complete treatise in this book on the subject of such

associated but distinct agencies would make dull reading, but perhaps a passing glance at some of them may prove interesting.

The Breed Societies. The main concern of every breed society is to foster in the minds of the rest of humanity the idea that their particular breed of cattle, or whatever animal it is, is the best in the world. In pursuit of their ideal they are tirelessly (one might say tiresomely!) diligent and surprisingly resourceful. Actually their concern is not really necessary, for the fortunate fact is that Scotland, by reason of the nature of its soil, climate and the sort of grass we grow, is by far and away the best stock-breeding country in the world. That is why shrewd men from the great ranching countries come to Scotland year after year and pay incredibly big prices for bulls of various breeds. Nor is this gold mine likely to peter out in a foreseeable future; for the other delightful truth is that in these great ranching countries, because of the deleterious effect on live-stock of climate and other conditions, a fresh infusion of the vigorous blood of the Scottish-bred bull is and will continue to be an annual necessity. In this connection, I remember in America some years ago visiting one of the big abattoirs and being treated to lunch by the management in the restaurant of their gigantic premises in Chicago. Including the then head of the firm there were about a dozen of us seated at a circular table. Suddenly, as the roast beef was being served, a peculiar silence became quite noticeable and developed into a strained atmosphere that I just could not understand. Then someone made an obvious effort at conversation and I started in to my roast beef— a noble helping equal to nearly half a dozen of our present weekly rations. To myself I soon had to confess that this lovely looking beef was a disappointment. In flavour it wasn't too bad—in fact it was all right; but it was mighty tough! Just at that moment came the shock: it was the President speaking:

"Say! Mr MacDonald, would you mind telling us straight just what you think of our roast beef?"

Having regard to the aforementioned self-communing, and to my innate horror of all but unavoidable lies, the question caused some momentary embarrassment, but, pulling myself together, I hedged brightly:

"Well, isn't that interesting?—that you should ask that question at the very moment I was thinking to myself 'What grand-flavoured beef!—beautiful!'"

"Yes," he said, "and what else?"

This was decidedly awkward for a guest. For three seconds I searched frantically for the right answer, but even that slight hesitation was enough. The great man came kindly though devastatingly to my relief: "Let me tell you what you'd say if you wasn't so darned polite; it would be: 'flavour beautiful, but *texture mighty tough.*'"

"No, sir!" he continued, "we've gotta face the fact. We have tried this breed and that. We have had all sorts of crosses. We have experimented with scores of varieties of grasses and in kinds and ways of feeding. No, sir! It's got us beat!—and the man who can put us on to the secret of prodoocing yon marly tender texture you get in your Scottish beef won't have to work no more!"

So let our Breed Societies be of good cheer.

.   .   .   .

The Highland and Agricultural Society of Scotland, as it was known for well over a hundred years, was founded at the instigation of an energetic and far-seeing Caithness man and ancestor of Sir Archibald Sinclair. The Society is best known to the public through the medium of its great show—"The Highland"—which moves round in rotation annually from one centre to another. But "The

Highland " is not merely a show of the cream of our farm live-stock and the latest agricultural machinery. It is also a big social event in the countryside, sometimes graced by the Royal Presence, and affording grand relaxation to the care-worn workers on the land.

In more recent times this Society has acquired some political force and thereby serves as a training ground for the Secretary of State for Scotland and the Society's principal officials in mutual toleration. Annually there is elected a new President, who in new-broom fashion sets about the business of making sweeping demands for governmental assistance for the industry. He can be a sore thistle in the thumb of the Secretary of State and his assistants and permanent officials whose primary duty is to say NO to all such demands. But, of course, both sides have to be polite ! And the way that works out as the year goes on provides an edifying example of the British way of government and people making the best of things: how the one has to be satisfied with less than his original demand and how the other finds it expedient to take some weight off the breeching. By the end of the tussle they have acquired much mutual respect, and each has a livelier appreciation of the other's difficulties.

.   .   .   .

The S.A.O.S., or to give its full title—Scottish Agricultural Organisation Society—has for about forty years been active in an effort to instil and foster the spirit of agricultural co-operation—particularly amongst small-holders ; and, considering the markedly anti-co-operative and pro-individualistic nature of the crofting population, S.A.O.S. are entitled to respect for the measure of success they have attained. That such small tenants should benefit substantially from co-operative action in purchasing their requirements and selling their produce seems theoretically watertight, but the fact remains that, for one of those psychological or other obscure reasons by which the Celt is apt to be guided in his practical affairs, he is not by instinct an ardent co-operator. Is that a fact to be deplored?—or is it not? I go no further than to suggest it might be an interesting study.

.   .   .   .

College of Agriculture. There are three of these : Edinburgh and East, Glasgow and West and Aberdeen and North of Scotland. Their function is purely educational. Each has its training centre, in association with the University, where young men and women study for degrees and diplomas in agriculture. To each College has been apportioned an area of country in which it has the responsibility for providing a full advisory service covering every aspect of Scottish agriculture and ensuring that the latest discoveries and developments in agricultural science are placed at the disposal of the practical man in the field. The usual team for each county, or part of some of the larger counties, is a County Agricultural Organiser (with sometimes an assistant) and a Dairy and Poultry Instructress. In addition, there is a service of " specialists " available from College Headquarters.

When first this service started—about the beginning of this century—there was a quite understandable tendency on the part of shrewd practical farmers to scoff at a service which savoured so strongly of lessons to granny in the art of sucking eggs. Dandies in breeches and polished shoes ! And henwives dressed like ladies ! But gradually it was borne in on the old farmer that the youths of the breeches brigade and the smartly-dressed henwives knew lots of things about farming that he didn't know—and would be much the better of knowing. It was a grudging recognition, but ultimately grew and spread all over the farming community. Now the best farmers normally seek the College man's advice on any problem that may arise. On the other hand the wise College man learns much of the more practical side of the business from his farmer friends—a mutual questing and learning relationship resulting in advantage to both.

CHAPTER X

Department of Agriculture : Some of its Doings and Troubles

The Department of Agriculture for Scotland is by far the largest of our family. It was born a Board in 1912, but (?) promoted to the status of Department in 1928. Travelling the country in its service as I did for many years I found it impossible to escape the feeling that in the opinion of the people the chief function of this great Department was the irritation of the rural community. Of course that was an exaggeration. All the same, by the very nature of its duties and of the powers statutorily conferred on it, some of the Department's operations were bound to cause considerable irritation to a number of people. For example, one of its primary duties was the provision of enlargements for existing small-holdings and the creation of new ones. That involved the procuring of land for such purposes, and to that end the Department was invested with powers to acquire land—compulsorily if need be. The shock caused by such a violation of the hitherto generally accepted notions of the sacred rights of private property may easily be imagined !

In a few cases hard-up landlords were glad to sell. In some cases they bowed to the inevitable. In many instances they strongly opposed the Department's schemes ; and almost without exception (but not quite) all cases developed into long legal battles over the question of compensation due to landlords and disturbed tenants. In addition to its power of acquiring land—that is, entering into full ownership—for its purposes, the Department also has power to impose schemes of new holdings and enlargements on land belonging to private owners, subject, of course, to the latter being adequately compensated. Now, one of our maybe illogical but certainly pronounced British characteristics is always to regard a Government Department as fair game when it comes to a question of extracting compensation. That despoiled landlords and disturbed tenants should be compensated adequately and even generously was very much in the minds of those of us who were directly concerned with land settlement schemes, and with a view to avoiding the expense of needless litigation our policy was to advise the Department to offer to settle privately at a figure considerably in excess of what the mere values in the case warranted. But for the first number of years most of such offers were scornfully rejected in favour of the chance of a higher award resulting from the legal battle. Nor did claimants often have reason to regret such recourse to the law. In cases where the Department did not purchase the land, but merely imposed a scheme on the private owner, a strong contention put forward by the latter in support of his claim for compensation was that, *because of his now having on his estate a number of small-holdings instead of a large farm, if and when he came to sell that part of the estate, he would not get so high a price for it in the market; there was thus a potential loss in selling value for which he must be compensated now.* The theory was that small-holders were undesirable tenants who would scare intending purchasers. In the final result the law and the arbiters supported that view and solemnly assessed the scare-value of small-holders on an estate at seven years' purchase. That is to say, that while a purchaser would be prepared to pay for the property a sum equal to say twenty-one years of its annual rental *as a farm*, he would not give more than fourteen rents for it as cut up into small-holdings, *e.g.*— take the case of a farm rented at £500.

Its selling value would be   £500 × 21 = £10,500
As small-holdings would be   £500 × 14 =   7,000

Thus leaving the landlord with a loss of   £3,500

Actually many thousands of pounds were awarded under that head of claim. Yet some years later, when a property which had been "mutilated" by small-holdings came to be sold, not only was there no loss to the landlord, but there was a very substantial profit. The demand for the small-holdings was so keen that in some cases they sold at rates 50 per cent. higher than that paid for large farms. After that experience amending legislation was introduced to bar such claims in future.

Another heavy item of claim was in respect of damage to sporting rights, especially where grouse-moors were involved. Here the general line was to assume that all small-holders were poachers, or at least careless of the value of the shootings to the landlord. Under the scheme they would have access to the moor to look after their sheep. There would be disturbance to birds by dogs and men. Nests would be destroyed. The grouse-bag would slump. The landlord would be ruined.

Despite carefully gleaned figures given in evidence to show that no such calamities resulted from small-holders having access to grouse-moors, for many years arbiters persisted in awarding substantial sums in compensation for a contingent loss which might never materialise; and it was probably the openly declared attitude of the late Sir Edgar Horne towards this matter which in the end was largely instrumental in disposing of the bogey.

At Lairg station one day, into my compartment in the south-going train came a large elderly gentleman with the assortment of bags, gun-cases, fishing rods and tackle and kindred impedimenta that usually denote the sporting gent. He was a stranger to me, but as he appeared to be quite genial I immediately set about satisfying natural curiosity.

And had he had a good holiday?

Indeed he had—a great holiday. He always enjoyed his stay in Sutherlandshire!

I agreed: indeed it was a grand sporting country! Had he been long in the north this time?

He had been for six weeks—and was still sore at having to tear himself away—but he would be back at Lairg again soon—perhaps within a month!

Good!—At Lairg? He wasn't by any chance Sir Edgar Horne of whom I had heard such a lot?

Indeed he was—and hoped his reputation wasn't as bad as all that! And who, might he ask, was I?

It was far from bad!—and I counted myself lucky to meet him—I was a minion of the Department of Agriculture—of whom he might not be enamoured but who might not be nearly as bad as they were painted. From then on we " southered " fine. At Inverness station, just as the train was about due to start, my companion, searching in his bags, got quite bothered about something. Though an abstemious man he required to have a small drop of stimulant occasionally. But he couldn't take naked whisky—and if he hadn't stupidly come away without a glass and without the usual diluent! While he was still deploring the oversight I bolted out at the door. Later I learned he had assumed it would be to speak to someone I must have seen on the platform.

As usual, the Edinburgh coach was right at the front of the train. I had to sprint back the full length of the platform. The guard had the green flag in hand ready for the starting wave.

" Don't let her go for two minutes," I pleaded with a desperate earnestness ; " something very important."

" But the time is up ! I can't wait . . . ! "

I waved back at him significantly.

Then to the lady in the refreshment room—" Two

tumblers and a bottle of soda ! " I gasped. " Quick, *please!* I'm going with this train."

She demurred about the glasses—but stemless glasses would do, or chipped ones—anything so long as the business end was intact !

She was a nice lassie, sympathetic and smart. As I rushed towards the rear of the train an angry but loyal guard waved the green flag and yelled at me to jump in—I could get along to the front by the corridor. Which I did as the train was actually under way.

Five minutes later I found my companion much distressed. My platform friend had delayed me too long ! I had missed the train ! Now he was happy again. He proceeded to tell me what he had been explaining when I ran out. No soda ! no glasses ! Most annoying.

" I sometimes carry a glass in my pocket," I said, pulling one out—and then another—and then the bottle of soda water from the hip pocket.

His eyes had opened wider with each extraction. " Good God ! Do you always go about with glasses and bottles of soda in your pockets ? "

Not always, I protested; just sometimes; and it was lucky I had them now !

After that we had a mutually delightful journey to Edinburgh, and it was then he told me of his experience with grouse-moors and crofters. It was to this effect:

When his London friends learned that he had bought an estate in the Highlands, having on it a large number of crofter tenants, they were sorry for him. It was a dreadful mistake ! These crofter fellows were incorrigible poachers. They would ruin his moor. He would require to get two or three extra gamekeepers at once; very expensive, and doubtfully effective, but without extra keepering the position was manifestly hopeless.

He had his doubts about all this, but could not help

being somewhat impressed by what those experienced friends said. However, he would go canny till he had put the matter to some test. For the first two seasons careful note was taken of the favourite nesting places and of where every bird was shot. A study of the collected facts showed that by far the best beats of the moor were those which formed the crofters' common pasture and to which they and their dogs and sheep and cattle had full right of access. He was so delighted at this emphatic repudiation of a belief widely held amongst tenants of grouse-moors that he invited all his crofter tenants to a supper and social evening where he had the pleasure of telling them the story of his friends' fears and his own apprehensions, and of his test and its wholly satisfactory result. That evening was the beginning of much friendly intercourse between landlord and tenants which promoted goodwill and mutual understanding and respect.

Nor did Sir Edgar often miss an opportunity of relating the story of his experience of crofters in relation to grouse.

Here have I been blethering quite a lot about my old Department, and still haven't said much about its manifold activities. Nor of these will I say more than that they extend to a concern to guide, control and encourage every conceivable measure calculated to promote the welfare of the industry, including the specialised activities of the subordinate or associated organisations aforementioned. But before leaving the subject there is one peculiar aspect that I just cannot resist having a look at; and if in doing so I give some of them a dig in the ribs, I trust any surviving old colleagues and friends will be big enough to take it in good part. I feel sure they will. Anyway, dash it all, I am entitled to my joke.

A simple-minded person might assume that a sound knowledge of agriculture would be an essential qualification for anyone charged with responsibility for directing the affairs of an agricultural department. But the matter is not so simple as that; and for long it has been the official view that for the satisfactory direction of a department's business in association with the responsible minister, administrative experience is the most essential qualification. There is an element of political discretion in the official view which may justify its general application. But, be that as it may, there is no doubt that at times a lack of understanding of the technicalities of the subject under discussion can be embarrassing and disadvantageous to the unfortunate official concerned; and personally, at meetings with farmers, I never ceased to admire and marvel at the dexterity and skill with which such officials, when all but bogged in bewildering idiomatic terminology, skated to safety over the thinnest of thin ice.

Perhaps it was the sheep department which caused their worst nightmares. And after all, what could the uninitiated make of an animal that might be one of so many things?—a lamb, a hogg, a gimmer, a maiden ewe, a ewe, a fine ewe, a yeld ewe, a cast ewe, a milled ewe, a dinmont, a wedder, a keb, a piner, a pallie, a peelie, a straggler, a tup, a top, a mid, a shott—and heaven knows how many more shapes that this blasted beast can assume! Worse still: the confounded things wouldn't stay put! It is fatal to assume that what is a gimmer this year must still be a gimmer next year. In all probability she will not—although confound it! she *may* remain a gimmer, but with the prefix " Eild "; and so on with those alarming and elusive female classes.

In face of such a fluid and treacherous nomenclature how on earth could anyone, whose knowledge of sheep was hitherto limited to the beast in cooked form, be expected to make head or tail of the matter or to check up on the honesty of the technical officer in charge of the farm?

I remember an early sheep-stock case which caused

much perturbation at head office. We had taken over a large sheep farm in Sutherland for the purpose of breaking it up into a number of new small-holdings and enlargements for several groups of existing crofts. As is usual in such cases, most of the old arable land that had lain uncultivated for many years as pasture for sheep would, under the new régime, form the arable land of the new holdings, with a consequent diminution in the number of sheep which could be kept, but with more than a compensating increase in crops and cattle and people. This meant that, after the small-holders had taken over the number of sheep which the diminished grazings would carry, there would be a surplus which must be sold off. But nearly all the farm leases in Sutherlandshire have their termination at a Whitsunday term; and it was at Whitsunday that we took over this place with its sheep-stock numbering nearly 5,000 head. It was at that same Whitsunday term the new holders and crofters got formal entry to the land and, " on paper " at least, took over their respective lots of the different classes of sheep.

But Whitsunday is just about the worst time for splitting up a sheep-stock or for disposing of a surplus. The lambs are then too young to be driven off their home hirsel or trucked to a sale—and in any case that is not the normal season for marketing ewes or lambs. So the holders and myself agreed that by far the most sensible plan would be to carry on the stock as an undisturbed unit till the back end when, lambs, cast ewes, wool, etc., having been duly disposed of at normal sales, a complete trading account could be prepared on a basis for a pro-rata allocation of profits and stock. With that in view we made at Whitsunday only a " paper " allocation of stock, and it was left to me to carry on in the management and prepare the statement for final settlement in November.

6

With so many new holders and resident crofters (in addition to the Department) as shareholders in the venture, anyone with knowledge of such matters can readily appreciate the highly complicated and delicate handling entailed in the preparation of a statement satisfactory to all parties. Here I need only say that for weeks of nights I sweated blood over it and was more than a little pleased with the final elucidation; dead sheep, lost sheep, sheep transferred to holders, lambs sold (tops, mids and shotts), ewes sold, (ditto and also broken-mouthed), wool sold (fleece, skins and broke), cost of fence repairs, marketing, clipping, dipping and all the rest of it worked out to the third decimal point per head of sheep. There it was; the perfect exposition that was bound to impress the fellows at head office with the manner of man its composer must be! . . . Well, they weren't favourably impressed at all. Indeed, I rather gathered that in so involved a series of intromissions they suspected there might well be the possibility of an opportunity for improbity. Of course they didn't quite put it that way; but I did receive on two sheets of foolscap no fewer than twenty-two demands for more light on specified portions of my masterpiece. The questions were neatly numbered down the left half of the page. Opposite was ample space for reply. I couldn't decide whether to meet this blow with tears or profanity. I know there was a little of the latter. Then I just laughed when I tumbled to it that what had inspired most of this catechism was the inability of the people at head office to make head or tail of the technical terms which of necessity bestrewed my report. One of the questions was priceless—and it was in my favour! Here it is:

" It is observed that at the Whitsunday valuation you reported having taken over 914 wedder lambs and 941 ewe lambs. You further reported on 6th June having taken over 12 additional lambs classed as ' stragglers,' which together make a total of 1,867 lambs taken over.

" It is further observed that according to the statements of your intromissions, the number of lambs sold, retained for holders and listed as dead, total 1,878—or 11 in excess of the number you took over. Please explain this discrepancy."

And I was cruel enough to write opposite that one just two words: " Grit ewes."

NOTE.—Grit ewe is the name applied to a ewe which has not yet lambed on the day of the valuation. I had duly listed such in my valuation report.

CHAPTER XI

Friendly Official—Modest Native

IN its earliest years—1912 to 1918—the Board of Agriculture for Scotland (as it then was) was assiduous in the work of creating new holdings and enlarging existing crofts: so much so, that for this purpose one large estate after another had been acquired at a rate which far exceeded the possible speed of settlement. As a result we had in hand during the years of the first world war a large number of farms and estates for whose management people like myself were held responsible. Under conditions obtaining at that time—war-time restrictions and an indoor clerical staff innocent of agricultural knowledge, but exasperatingly ingenious in putting spokes in practical people's wheels!—it was bad enough to be landed with the ordinary work of management in addition to the essential work of interviewing applicants for holdings, framing new schemes for development and supplying munitions for frequent legal battles between the Board and landlords ; but when on top of this was added the responsibility for keeping accurate accounts to be rendered monthly, the thing became a nightmare to most of us whose skill in accountancy was not our strong point. Every month it was a nightmare trying to get the darned things straight; nor did it help to know that if one did make a mistake it might be a year after the event that head office financial pundits would discover it and call for an explanation. It was terrible to be going in constant dread of being shown up as a thief or embezzler. At long last my often-urged request that someone from head office should pay periodic visits to give a hand with accounts at the provincial offices was given effect to. To most of the out-door officers this leg-along was a mighty relief. Incidentally, the job of travelling to the provinces became highly popular amongst those of the indoor staff with any pretensions to a knowledge of the obscure art of accountancy. For such slaves of the pen it was sheer heaven to know that to-morrow they would discard the shiny blue suit. They would habit themselves like men; for three to four days, perhaps for a week, they would breathe the untainted air of the countryside; they would come into close and prideful contact with stots and sheep; maybe even the honey-scented breath of the heather might permeate their lungs. Of course, they would have to come back! But they would come back with the tan of the sun on their faces, the song of the burn in their ears and a joy and hope in their hearts that would enable them to thole their chains till the next time.

That was how my old friend and colleague Gemmell felt that time he went to check up on the accounts at the Portree office. Maybe he had caught a trout or two, also; I wouldn't put it past him. But, anyway, he was enjoying himself—as he has a grand capacity for doing. Even when the joke is against himself no one enjoys it better— as I think you will sense from the fact that it was from himself I got this one.

On the way back from Portree, in consequence of a not unusual disaccord of boat and train movements, he found himself at Kyle of Lochalsh with a couple of hours to spare before the south-going train would start. But it was a grand day! And there were so many things to see from yon lovely view-point in front of the hotel. Across the shining water rose the frowning hills of Skye. Down at sea-level that gem of Highland hamlets that is Kyleakin. The ruins of Caisteal Moile, onetime stronghold of the MacKinnons, who it is said used it as a base from which to sally forth to demand toll from ships passing up and down the waters of the Kyle. For centuries Caisteal Moile has been a roofless ruin of massive walls and gables, seemingly on the point of disintegrating and tumbling into the sea, but still held together by a mixture that can be no ordinary mortar! And the ferry-boats, shuttling this way and that, packed with strangers from the south seeking the quiet of a Highland holiday; the gracefully gliding gulls—when they weren't in screaming squabble over the ownership of a discarded herring or some other fishy titbit. Then in the village itself the shops with their open doors and unhurried customers. Huge rolls of home-spun, in golden crotal and the blue of the sky, stood invitingly out in the roadway in front of the shops—at three-and-six a yard !

Having feasted his fill on such scenes and with still an hour to spare he set off for an inland walk. Soon he found himself passing not far from an old white-whiskered man working at the peats. With the infectious sociability born of pleasant contact with the country my friend hailed the ancient:

" It's a grand day for the peats ! "

" It iss that: och yiss, a peautiful tay," the old gentleman agreed. " And dit you hear the news of the war? "

In those days our latest war news came through the medium of a telegram displayed in the post office window. At once my friend diagnosed this to be the case of an old man anxious on account of a son or grandson away at the war. He had read the telegram at Kyle and passed on the gist of it to the dear old fellow.

" And how are they getting on at Galipolly? " inquired the native.

That's where the son or grandson is, the informer was convinced; and he was sorry he could give no more reassuring report of that sector of the struggle. " But mind you," he added, " it isn't easy for our fellows to get at the Turks, and it's very difficult for our ships to get up behind him through the Dardanelles."

" Aye, aye ? " obviously much interested.

" Yes: you see it's like this ": and with his Edinburgh walking-stick my friend sketched on the road a rough plan of the Dardanelles and proceeded to enlighten ignorance. " The Turks have a fort with heavy guns right here " (a dot on the road), " and then another on the other side here " (another dot), " another here, and here."

The interest evinced by his audience encouraged him to give a full and graphic explanation of the difficulties then besetting the British Forces in their attempt to overcome the Turk.

" Yiss, yiss ! I am understanding it fine ! And you will haff been oucht there yourself ? " the old man asserted rather than inquired.

" No, no ! " (modestly, but proud of the compliment). " I just saw it on a map in the newspaper."

" Well, well now ! Inteet, you made a ferry goot chop of it ! " came the compliment.

" Oh, thank you ! I'm very glad I helped you to understand."

" Yiss, yiss ! you make it ferry goot inteet—chist as like it iss ass anysing ! "

It was only then a glimmer came to the instructor—but no ! impossible . . .

" You—you—you were never out there yourself ? " he ventured incredulously.

Then, very modestly, " Och inteet yiss, I wass oucht there when I wass a young man. I went up the Strights seven times, but I only came down seex times because the last time I wass up fever broke oucht in the sheep and I was put into a hospital in Constantinople and I wass seex weeks there and then travelled by a traine to jine another sheep at Fiume. You will haff heard of Fiume ? "

CHAPTER XII

Land Court: Constitution and Peregrinations—Oath
Evasions—Waterloo!—Economy in Words—The Right
Time—Biblical Quotations

AND now about that august body, the Scottish Land
Court. In the main its function may be described as
"judicial." It acts as judge, arbiter and friendly inter-
mediary in the wide variety of cases of dispute, disagree-
ment or uncertainty in regard to things agricultural
which have a habit of cropping up between owners of
land and their tenants. I shall not attempt to enumerate
the cases of different type and nature that come, or may
come, before this Court in the course of a year—they
are practically innumerable. But whatever the point at
issue, the Court's solemn responsibility is to keep the
balance even.

Its roots go back to 1886, in which year, as a result of
a decade of alarming agrarian unrest throughout the
Highlands, there was put on the statute book that measure
which has so crucially and intimately affected the lives
and circumstances of our Highland people—The Crofters'
Act. From then on, all differences of opinion as to whether
the rent of a croft was fair or whether a crofter could be
removed from his holding, with or without compensation
in respect of permanent improvements he may have
carried out on it, ceased to be a matter for wrangling and
ill-feeling between factor and crofter. For under the
new Act was set up a judicial tribunal called the Crofters'
Commission before whom all such disputes could be
brought, and to whom each party could give relative
evidence on oath. And the Commission, having considered the evidence and inspected the subjects, duly
issued their findings and pronounced their decision—and
that was that.

Under the wise administration of the Commission and the protection afforded by the Act, crofters proceeded apace with improvements to land and buildings, and the " Land Question," so long the source of bitter feelings and conflict in the Highlands, gradually lost its venom. In course of time the advantages of the new régime became so obvious all over the area to which the Crofters' Act applied—Shetland, Orkney, Caithness, Sutherland, Ross, Inverness and Argyll—that in 1911 further legislation was enacted which provided for the extension of similar and additional advantages to the whole of Scotland. This was the Small Landholders' (Scotland) Act which gave birth to the Board of Agriculture for Scotland and substituted the Scottish Land Court for the Crofters' Commission.

The present authorised establishment provides for five Members of Court of whom one—a senior member of the Scottish Bar of not less than ten years standing—shall be chairman. The ordinary Members of Court are deemed to be men with a wide knowledge of agricultural practice and values, and one of them must be a Gaelic speaker. In control of the office and staff there is the Principal Clerk to the Court.

The present set-up is:

> Chairman and three Members.
> Principal Clerk.
> Three Legal Assessors.
> One Surveyor.
> One Accountant.
> One Keeper of the Rolls.
> One Grazings Officer.
> Four Clerical Officers.
> Two Typists.
> Two Messengers.

And—I am bound to say it—an astonishingly small team to overtake the volume of highly responsible and delicate work which they are called upon to do.

To each ordinary member is allocated a section of the country within which (with the assistance of his legal assessor when necessary) he normally deals with and decides all cases that may arise. Against such a decision, though, there is the much prized right of appeal. The Chairman along with the other two Members of Court and the Principal Clerk hear appeals. Their decision is final and can only be referred to the Court of Session in a stated case on a point of law.

In its high degree of mobility the Land Court is unique. Instead of hauling far-away applicants into Edinburgh to have their cases heard—and thereby involving them in considerable expense and inconvenience—this most sensibly designed tribunal goes out all over the country to issue its decrees and dispense its justice; sometimes at the local Sheriff Court, but it may be the village hall, a school, a crofter's kitchen, a barn, a byre or even a stance on the open moor which serves the Scottish Land Court's purpose and is for the nonce imbued with all the dignity and solemnity of a Court of Session. The mere process of putting a witness on oath goes a long way in producing this atmospheric metamorphosis and when supported by the awe-inspiring effect of the Chairman's gorgeous robe the transformation is complete.

Not that the Highlander, as a rule, is anxious to take the oath. Sometimes, indeed, he refuses to do so even when warned that by so doing he may be prejudicing his case. It has been suggested to me that this reluctance is due to his awareness that the disclosure of the truth, the whole truth, and nothing but the truth, might not be to his advantage anyway. But I incline to the view that the real explanation lies in the fact that the mere extraction of so solemn an undertaking has in it the insulting inference that otherwise he might tell lies! Times without number I have seen and heard my brother Celts instinctively and anxiously seeking to evade the awful affirmation in the oath. Many of them just slither the essential words, hoping that it will be attributed to a defective knowledge of English; and one venerable old gentleman did it so well that he actually got off with " the truse, the whole truse and everysing but the truse! "

Neither could one fail to admire the ease and dignity with which many of those who appeared before the Court conducted themselves; a circumstance due in part perhaps to the reputation of the Court for giving every suppliant's case patient and fair consideration, but certainly largely the result of independence of outlook and self-confidence characteristic of a people living in security on the land.

Away back in the eighteen eighties at a hearing before the Crofters' Commission, the Chairman—Sheriff Brand —was so much impressed by the quality and clarity of the evidence given by a very old man in English, despite his limited knowledge of that language, that at its conclusion he felt it incumbent on him to express his appreciation and thanks. He added: "And it is all the more remarkable that such evidence should come from a man of your years—for you are not now so young as you once were, Mr Cameron! "

" Och indeed, no sir," Mr Cameron agreed with a smile.

" Just how old are you, Mr Cameron, can you tell me? " inquired his Honour.

" Och, chist *me* to-day, *Waterloo* to-morrow! " came the cryptic reply.

In another chapter I tell in some detail of the result of taking evidence in Gaelic and having it translated by an interpreter. Recently it was rumoured in official circles that the necessity for having a Gaelic-speaking member of the Land Court no longer exists. With that I do not agree; and that not merely because of the indignant protests which would certainly come if the suggestion were given effect to. While it is true that a good knowledge of English is now widespread throughout the Highlands—better English, indeed, than you will find in any other rural community in the British Isles—the fact remains that when it comes to making a verbal statement before a tribunal like the Land Court, the native Gaelic speaker prefers to do so in the native tongue. Thus it is that every now and again, particularly in the Islands, a witness asks to be permitted to give evidence in Gaelic. Nor is this surprising. He could probably prepare a *written* statement of his case in flawless English, but his evidence must be given by word of mouth—and that is a very different matter. Besides, on the tongue of the master, the finer shades of expression in the Gaelic can be so much more effectively applied to his purpose.

At a sitting of the Court in Skye only a few years ago the Chairman was somewhat surprised when a well-dressed young lady, who was known to have lived for several years in Glasgow, asked to be permitted to give her evidence in Gaelic. In reply to his Lordship's suggestion that in her case such a procedure might not be necessary, she explained that while it might not be altogether necessary, she still felt she would be able to give her evidence more adequately and clearly in Gaelic. She did not wish to inconvenience the Court in any way, but if her evidence was to be taken in English could she have the Court's permission when answering questions to refer to a written statement in English which she had prepared in anticipation of such an eventuality?

Not only was the desired permission granted but the witness was invited to read the statement if she so desired. She did; and that statement could not have been bettered by a D.Litt., LL.B.

As the story in another chapter shows, when an interpreter is brought into a case the opportunity for supplementing exchanges between interpreter and witness is quite considerable. It's all very well to have fired at you a crisp question in a foreign tongue which in the mind of the originator needs a " yes " or " no " reply! But a " yes " or " no " is terribly committal! A Highland gentleman must have delicate regard to the dreadful possibility of unwittingly stating—on oath!—what may not be quite true by so drastically limiting his reply. So, even when he may have a shrewd idea of the purport of the question in its original form, he must ask his friend the interpreter for elucidation. And his fellow Gael, quick to appreciate the need for such, proceeds to supply it. But the elucidation, because of the wealth of nuances in the language of the Garden, in all probability discloses within it matter for further grave consideration which in the interest of absolute truth must be investigated. So it is that in such cases the Court or an arbiter or legal gentleman is apt to conclude either that the witness is a downright twister, or that as a medium for concise expression the Gaelic language is of low degree—and that possibly there is an element of both responsible for the protracted procedure! But, of course, so uncharitable a conclusion is rooted in ignorance.

I recall one Chairman of the Land Court who was profoundly sceptical of the necessity for those five minute conversations between witness and interpreter which were ultimately translatable in a syllable. Nor did his Lordship miss many opportunities of twitting some of us about the the shortcomings of the Celt and his language. But one day we got our own back on him—in full! This same Chairman, anxious to ensure that applicants should not merely understand what the Court's decision in the case was, but also the reasons that led to it, not infrequently announced the decision from the bench and then proceeded to give the reasons annexed at considerable length! On this occasion the decision was to the effect that the applicant (who, through an interpreter, had pressed hard for a certain advantage) had failed to make good and was thus left in *status quo*. . . . No doubt with a view to blunting the sting of disappointment, the Chairman launched what developed into a long-winded and somewhat tedious explanation of causes. The interpreter, who had heard the essential verdict and was expected to garner a few of the crumbs of comfort for passing on to the applicant at the finish, unfortunately fell sound asleep at an early stage of the monologue. Not until the silence which followed its termination did he waken up! His Lordship was waiting for the interpreter to administer the bitter pill with the sugar coating. The interpreter rose to his feet, adjusted his spectacles, looked solemnly towards the unsuccessful applicant and said, " *Thà thu mar bhà thu.*" * He then bowed respectfully to his Lordship and resumed his seat!

No one who visits a Celtic community even for a short period can fail to notice—and envy—the philosophic decorum of the people in their attitude towards Time; for to them that rushing to do this or that with the unseemly haste so characteristic of slave-driven city people, whose lives and actions are governed and inhibited by the blaring of factory horns and railway time-tables, merely discloses an irreverent lack of appreciation of one of Nature's greatest gifts to man. As if Time were a commodity that came gushing through a tap from a cistern

* Highland-English equivalent : " You *are* as you *was*."

that will soon run dry! No wonder, therefore, that a stranger desirous of fixing up a meticulous holiday itinerary during his visit to the Highlands may find the Celt somewhat elusive; but to conclude from such evidence that laziness and lack of business acumen are qualities inherent in the Highlander is often but evidence of the visitor's less mature philosophy.

Even people who ought to know better, fresh from the stir of the city, are apt for a day or two to forget to tune in again to the serener tempo of the north. There was yon time the flight of the aeroplane from Renfrew to the island was delayed by fog and I was getting apprehensive about the possibility of being late for a sitting of the Court. On arrival at the hotel (several miles from the place of meeting) I was indiscreet enough to voice that fear to the hotel-keeper. My host looked at me pityingly. Surely I should know the islands better than that!—as if an hour here or there mattered!

I apologised; but after all, punctuality had some legal significance where the Land Court was concerned, I pleaded.

And when I got there (he ridiculed) I would probably find they were going by the sun and I would be far too early.

He declared I was no better than an Englishman he had recently staying in the hotel. The English visitor had a friend staying in private lodgings some miles away. One day the pair arranged that on the morrow they would go out with the land-lines for a fry of codlings. They would meet at a bay, where there was a boat and tackle, at eleven o'clock next morning. It was to be a grand outing and was much in the mind of the hotel guest that evening. He would have to be up in good time and warned several people of the necessity for an early knock.

But that night there seemed to be an unholy conspiracy against the poor man:

Item. The hotel-keeper hadn't possessed a watch since the beginning of the war.

Item. Every one of the dozen or so clocks decorating the various mantelpieces and lobbies had observed a profound silence for years.

Item. In his excitement the visitor had over-wound his wrist watch so that it had stopped at the moment of winding and he hadn't noticed.

Item—and last straw: the wireless battery had run done.

Not that this row of unfortunate circumstances disturbed in the slightest degree the tranquillity of the hotel-keeper and his staff. But to the fisherman it was very disturbing indeed. He might be far too early. But he might be too late! Good heavens! What a place! And nobody seemed to bother, and their repeated assurance, " Och! you'll be there time enough, right enough," was just an aggravation. He had a hurried breakfast—or at least as hurried as breakfasts happen there—and set off for the rendezvous in a mood mixed of annoyance and apprehension.

Ha! Here was someone coming who might have the desired information! It was an elderly Celt, ample in form, in blue guernsey and sea-boots, and in contemplative mood smoking his pipe.

" Good morning," said the Englishman.

" Good morning," cordially responded the Celt, but making to pass on, still deep in contemplation.

" Excuse me, but can you tell me the time? " anxiously inquired the Englishman.

" Time! " said the Celt, jolted out of his reverie and desperately pulling his beard in anxiety to oblige the stranger. " Time? Time? I think it's *Tuesday*, isn't it? "

In the hearing of a case a certain Chairman of the Court was always quick to seize any opportunity of quoting scripture to illustrate a point in the matter under discussion. On one occasion in Lewis whilst a venerable Islander was giving evidence his Lordship had freely indulged this pet propensity. But it would seem that his recourse to Holy Writ was more frequent than accurate. For a time the witness suffered in silence but at last was goaded into protest:

" If your Lordship will be for using the Holy Word at all in a case of this kind it would be better if you used it correctly. Indeed, I am thinking myself you would be wiser to take any quotations you need from your law books, with which no doubt you will be better acquainted than you are with your Bible."

CHAPTER XIII

(Being Extracts from Diary)

River Inspection—A Wet Day

For nearly a week we have had the most glorious of summer days. It's grand to see the early morning light stealing over the whin bushes of the Braids, as I am lucky to be able to do, from my bedroom window; a glimmering grey at first, but quickly changing through varying hues of indescribable beauty till at last the sun himself appears in regal splendour to proclaim another day.

There is endless interest, too, in observing the doings of the denizens of the rookery near the tennis courts at the Braid Burn; for, be it fair weather or foul, and whatever the season of year, just about half an hour before sunrise out sally the crows in their daily search for breakfast; they know precisely, too, where to go for the best rations.

Every spring and early summer there is a recurring battle of wits between crow and farmer for the potato sets which the latter has planted to produce that year's crop and which the former strives to steal as his favourite morning titbit. At the farmer's most realistic tattie bogle the crow—so to speak—soon puts his claw to his beak. During reasonable daytime hours the farmer usually has the upper hand: what between dykes and hedges behind which he can sneak in on them, and that grossly unfair and fatal instrument he puffs at them with such terrifying noise, a potato field is a chancy place for crows in daytime. So Mr Crow, wise by experience (and without a single " caw " !) slips over to snatch his favourite breakfast while his arch-enemy is still abed.

For his protein diet the crow has a passion for Leatherjacket, an ugly grub begotten of the harmless-looking

Daddy-Long-Legs, which in dry weather plays the very devil with the young oat-crop after old lea. The war-time plough-up of golf courses and other tough old pasture land made high holiday for the crows in their neighbourhood, for there, under the surface clods left by the harrows, are leather-jackets in their thousands; and there will be the crows in regiments, morning, noon and evening, turning over clod after clod with their bills as expertly as you could with your fingers and gobbling down the grub in incredible quantity. A few of the more sporting farmers allow in their reckoning a spot of credit to the crow on this account—but I'm afraid the great majority remember only the stolen potatoes!

To-day has been yet another of those lovely days. It's rather interesting to realise how many good days we do have when one begins to take note of them—and it is also interesting to note how prone many of us are to remember only the bad days: a sort of dour Calvinistic trait which seeks joy in gloom. One morning not so long ago there was a deluge of rain being driven along by a gusty wind as I entered the office. Now, while we did have rather more than a fair share of rude weather earlier on, that was positively the first rain we had had after a week of genial sunshine. Yet the greeting of a colleague that morning was: " Isn't this awful! Rain! Rain! every blooming day without a halt! "

Well! but as I started to tell, to-day really has been one of those lovely days that live in the memory; a blazing sun, a blue, blue sky artistically flecked with white wispy clouds, and just that breath of cooling breeze. On such a morning we step out blithely, even on city pavements that but lead to the shop or office.

But och! if only we could be out among the broom bushes on the brae or picking our steps along the banks of a moorland burn and here and there stopping to try to tempt the trout from beneath its green banks! And yet, look you at what can happen!

Wednesday—that was the day before yesterday—it was just another such day as this. The Court were " sitting " in state, uncomfortably dolled up in dark and ancient garments and with a richly robed and bewigged chairman, all complete. Learned Counsel, also dressed in the sombre habiliments of their sordid trade, were doing their clever best to get their own witnesses to say the right thing in support of their case and to get the witnesses on the other side to corroborate; so that the " learned judges " were in danger of being bamboozled by being pulled this way and that. All through that weary day of trying to reconcile irreconcilables the sun was high in the heavens and the earth was gay—and this lugubrious investigation might go on for days!

In the late afternoon, before rising, and as by a common impulse, there was a whispered consultation on the bench: what about going to *see* this wretched river that we had heard so much about, which had or had not been so efficiently cleaned that the adjacent farm lands had or had not been improved? Never was decision more quickly taken : we would go and see the *locus* to-morrow. That was the obvious thing to do; we could then listen to and talk about the case intelligently. Splendid! that suited everybody. Of course, nothing was said about the joy of walking among the corn and barley rigs or of strolling by the side of the murmuring river in the glorious summer's sunshine, but anticipation ran joyfully, if silently, high.

Next morning (yesterday as ever was!) a first glance through the window made it all too obvious that the " sunstoker " was on strike. A smooth rain was falling and the sky was leaden grey.

Ach! but wasn't that the usual prelude to a bright and

bonnie day? It would clear up by the time we reached the rendezvous by the river; so we ate heartily and hurried to the station in high hope.

After an hour in the train, learning from the daily press of the singular lack throughout the world of that brotherhood of man which our national poet was so optimistic about, we got out at a station where cars were waiting to take us for the out—ahem—inspection.

It was too bad that the sun had not yet come out; in fact there was quite a business-like shower as we drove off.

Passing by the farms we could see that much rain had fallen in the night: field after field of timothy was as flat as if steam-rollered. Unfortunately for us the wheat and oats, as well as the thistles and couch and knot-grass, were still standing sturdily erect, and as we began our inspection, believe me, every blade of grass—and oats and wheat and thistle—kepped its ain drap o' dew!

Being British we couldn't retreat, so we plodded on and on, weary and uncommonly wet, for over two hours. Learned Counsel, somewhat inadequately clothed, were there in force, and manfully stuck to their unusual job. The non-technical side of the Court, including the Chairman, shrewdly saw there was no necessity for *them* to inspect the river; so they discreetly retired to a barn while the heroes bent to their task.

By noon we concluded we were as wet as we could possibly be—and, right enough, we were far from dry. But most things are relative. Just then a black overhead cloud that we hadn't particularly noticed had a stab of lightning through it—and down it came in torrents. We were still half a mile from the cars. Between us and them was a perfect jungle of water-laden cereals and weeds to negotiate. Were we wet?

At the nearest hostelry—six miles away—even some of the semi-teetotallers didn't shrink from the fire-water which we coaxed from the bar-lady at five shillings a glass.

Now the sun is resplendent again; the larks will be singing, and the cereals will be whispering lovingly in the gentle breeze—while we again sit in the Court listening to the lawyers!

Yet, we are not sorry—and we *are* more intelligent. And after all, whatever unkind things we may say about our Scottish weather we cannot say that it lacks variety.

CHAPTER XIV

(Being Extracts from Diary)

Flying to Barra—The Importance of a Will

LAST Tuesday, having breakfasted in Glasgow, we left at 8.25 in a bus for Renfrew. Scottish Airways have fairly spruced things up. No more standing in a draughty shed waiting to be weighed: a polite official invites you to use one of several well-upholstered chairs and couches in a luxurious lounge. This fosters a feeling of affluence which tends to soothe the sore of having had to part with all of ninety shillings as the price of personal transport from Renfrew to Barra—not that I should grumble! Hasn't His Majesty's Lord Treasurer's Remembrancer for nearly forty years faithfully reimbursed me for such expenditure? Moreover, I felt quite guilty in the knowledge that the rate for self and luggage worked out at 4½d. per lb., while the rate for a nice wee seven-stone wifie who crossed by the same plane must have been about 1od.

It was her first flight, but she soon forgot her first-flight apprehensions in the wonder of gliding smoothly over strange-looking towns and toy farmsteads, and then over loch and mountain and deep blue sea.

There—there near the north end of Jura is the swirling Corryvreckan; and there, right below us is Iona, the Scottish very cradle of Christianity.

In exactly an hour she was again on solid earth on the Reef of Tiree. Then off again on a final flip and there she was, in an hour and a half from Renfrew on the snow-white cockle-strand of her native Barra! *Dhia gle mise!* And then from old friends those words of welcome that are so warm on the Gaelic tongue. Here for a fortnight the soot and fog of the city are forgotten in the joy of the silver strand, in the greens and blues and purples of the ever-changing seas. . . .

Oh, yes! There will be a bit of a shower there sometimes, too; and there will be times when the wind will blow the blue colour from the seas that will roll and roar and burst heavens high against the rocks. But isn't that, too, the grand sight?

. . . .

Every year there comes from the Highlands to the Land Court in Edinburgh a crop of requests for local investigation of complaints and difficulties, and " craves " for their settlement. A frequent cause of trouble is the question of march fences or the boundaries of the croft. Pity you the man who, either innocently or covetously, when laying down his crops encroaches by even a foot-breadth on his neighbour's land! Nor is the question so easily settled as one might suppose, for the march may be up to a mile long and anything but a straight line or on level ground. What between the ups and the downs of it, the little rocks and the big rocks that intersect the alleged line of boundary, and the *feanagan* and *baic-mona* (lazy-beds and peat-hags) that abut on it from every angle of the compass, the man who has to decide between the hotly hostile disputants would need to be a bit of a Solomon as well as a surveyor. On one occasion when, as usual, the truth got thoroughly bogged in a mire of contradictory verbal evidence, it was decided to inspect the *locus* in the hope of getting some light there—one witness having sworn that he knew the boundary well, and could show it to the Court by walking it from end to end. So out to the open went the Court and the crowd. In such circumstances it had been Mr Norman Reid's custom to remind the boundary-walker that although not now in the witness-box he was still on oath. This time by a mischance he forgot at the outset to give the usual warning. After the man had walked about a hundred yards—in a direction that presumably raised some doubt in the judge's mind—Norman remembered the omission and immediately corrected matters with an admonitory bawl that sounded like the island's fog-horn:

" Sandy! Sandy! Mind now! With every step you take your feet are ON OATH! "

Then in a case where the crofter dies intestate there is the question of deciding who has the right of succession. For the information of those who do not know (and there are many even in Scotland!), let me explain very briefly that one of the great features of the Crofters' Act of 1886 (now incorporated under the more comprehensive title The Small Landholders' (Scotland) Acts, 1886 to 1931, which have done more for the Highlands than any other legislative measure in the past hundred years) is the peculiar form of tenure which gives the holder the undisturbable right to remain in occupation during his life-time and the right to pass on a similar right to anyone within a specified circle of relationship. But if he wants to be sure that the person of his choice shall succeed he had better do something about it: he should either " assign " the holding or " bequeath " it. The former process requires the sanction of the Land Court and results in the assignee taking occupation of the holding while the old holder is still living, but usually with a friendly understanding that he will stay in his old home and get bed and board—and respect and *ceilidh* rights and privileges till the end of his day. But here's the rub! The crofter who philosophically contemplates his own demise and makes sensible arrangements for the time subsequent to that event is rather exceptional. In fact the great majority of crofters are most reluctant to make a will or an assignation, and most of them never do—often with lamentable consequences to those whom they most love. Take the sort of case that not infrequently comes before the Land Court.

Donald, the holder, and Mary his wife have been in the place since they married. They have suffered sore bereavement by the death of their only child. They are now middle-aged; there will be no more family. But they are still both hale and hearty and have many years of happy companionship to look forward to. Then Donald, out at the lobster creels, gets soaked to the skin, catches a cold which develops into pneumonia—and Mary, still scarcely realising the fact, is already Donald's widow.

Perhaps the greatest mitigation of her grief comes from the knowledge that at least she has her beloved home— the home that was Donald's father's and grandfather's and great-grandfather's before him—and the house that Donald had improved and made so cosy after their marriage so many years ago. Nor is she quite empty-handed, for Donald was a hard-working provident man; so that between his lobsters and herring-fishing, and the Government subsidies of £10 per acre for potatoes, £3 an acre for rye, £7 per cow and stirk (they had two head of each) and seven and sixpence a head for their twenty sheep, and Mary's own earnings from the world-famous Harris tweed, there was the tidy sum of £700 in the bank. Moreover, her favourite nephew from the croft on the other side of the bay—young Donald who had always been so mindful of herself and Donald, helping them with the work on the croft and with the sheep—would look after her affairs; and she would see to it that the croft would go to him after her day—*a laochan!*

So Mary settles down to make the best of what is left to her in life.

But within a month comes a shock in the form of a letter from a lawyer:

" Dear Madam,

" Acting on the instruction of Mr John MacEachan, 87 Millburn Street, Glasgow, I now beg to intimate to you as relict of the late Donald MacEachan that my client has lodged with the Scottish Land Court an application for an Order finding and declaring that he is heir-at-law of the said Donald MacEachan.

" As there does not appear to be any question of my client's right to succeed, and as he intends to take early personal occupation, I shall be glad to learn that you can make arrangements to quit the holding at an early date—and in any case not later than the term of Martinmas next."

" What lawyer's nonsense is this? " Mary asked indignantly of young Donald, but with a mind ill at case.

Young Donald has to confess that he does not know—but surely it *must* be nonsense—didn't the croft belong to Uncle Donald? And wasn't it him that built the new house—and wasn't Aunty Mary going to have what belonged to her man?

" Of course the croft was his; and wasn't it himself that lifted the new house so that I would have a nice home to come to; and it was Donald that made the garden and put up the fences—and all that was Donald's is mine! This letter, and that about Johnnie MacEachan must be a sort of cruel joke."

But poor Mary soon learns from the Land Court (before whom she had laid her trouble) that it isn't nonsense but sound law !—just an example of the application of the law of primogeniture. A man's widow is not his heir-at-law. As compared with the heir-at-law she has only limited rights of participation in his estate; and that, in the case of a crofter's widow, does not include the right of succession to the croft—unless her man has willed it to her. Donald had not done so—and that was the cause of all this heart-breaking trouble. Had Mary's son lived *he* would have succeeded as heir-at-law of his father; as it was, there was no doubt at all that Johnnie MacEachan (a son of a brother of Donald's) was heir-at-law, and as such entitled to get possession of the croft.

Nor is the law such a " hass " in this respect as might at first appear. For instance, suppose Donald Mac-Eachan had not been so lucky in his selection of a wife: suppose his wife had turned out a tartar or thoroughly bad egg (that does happen occasionally and there are many instances of a crofter deliberately " willing " the croft past such a wife); the sort of rank outsider that it would have grieved the heart of everyone in the Mac-Eachan family, male and female, to see established for life in their ancestral home—and with the right to pass it on, *not* necessarily to a MacEachan but to another of her own execrable brood! The thing is unthinkable! so into operation comes the law of primogeniture.

On the other hand there is legal protection and justice for the like of Mary in the Intestate Husbands' Estate (Scotland) Act, 1911-19, which provides that, in the event of there being no family and the total value of the estate not exceeding £500, the widow has the right of succession to the croft. And of course Mary's own man had it in his power all along to make sure that she would never be put out of her home—Och! if Donald had only the sense and decision to make a will, but he didn't—and he left more than £500 and so Mary was disinherited!

CHAPTER XV

Hill Farming—Road Hogs—The Hirsel—The Year's
Round—Snow Storm—A Man's Job—Harvest of the Hills

SOME of my hill farming friends may wonder why I write
this chapter at all. Well, they can skip it. But the fact
remains that things which to them must seem but the
very ordinary A B C of their lives (and therefore not worth
writing about) are to the majority of " outsiders "
involved in mystery and full of intriguing interest. How
often have I not seen (in days of plenty petrol) visitors
to our Scottish Highlands or the Borders enjoying for the
first time the glorious sensation of haring along a moorland road, with the honey scent of heather going like
wine to their heads, and with not a human being or even
a house in sight to break the serenity of the hills? Only
an occasional sheep, maybe with her lamb, by the roadside
or quietly browsing on the brae face and emphasising the
essential rusticity and peace; and just then!—a screech
of brakes and a sudden swerve—too late to avert tragedy:
a mother ewe or her baby or both horribly mutilated and
wriggling piteously to death. It takes a hardened motorist
to contemplate such with indifference. I have met some,
but thank goodness they are rare. The ordinary decent
man is acutely distressed, and if only he had a real
appreciation of the enormity of what he has done, surely
never again would he be so careless as to allow such a
thing to happen. Unfortunately, though, of the art and
intricacy of hill farming many of our summer visitors
are profoundly ignorant. Of the general extent of sheep-
raising in Scotland or of its importance to the country
they have but the faintest conception. It might surprise
such people to know that of the nearly 7,000,000 sheep
now in Scotland, about 4½ millions are bred and reared

on hill land, or " mountain and heath " as it is described in the official documents. Over 40,000 farmers and small-holders are in this industry—considerably more than half of all the agricultural tenants in Scotland—and the individual interest varies from around 10,000 to less than 10 head of sheep. Thus the capital value of sheep-stock on our hills must be in the neighbourhood of £20,000,000, and when to that is added the value of farm and croft equipment in the way of houses, steadings, fanks, fences, etc., some idea may be had of the substantial nature of the industry as a whole and of its vital interest to those who make their living in it. Actually, there are people so ignorant as to have the vague idea that that sheep they have killed by their speeding car is just one of those scattered beasts they see on the hillsides and probably not owned by anyone in particular! But, indeed, it has an owner who will be definitely out of pocket by its death; and a local shepherd could tell at a glance at the " keels " and " buists " and " lug-marks " not only the name of its owner and his farm, but its age and the very hirsel of that farm to which it belongs.

For the business of hill farming is not the haphazard thing that so many people imagine it to be. Indeed, there are hazards in plenty, but the farm and stock are run to a pattern and on a definite system, disregard of which would soon bring chaos and disaster. To get a rough idea of the set-up and rhythm on a hill farm perhaps the simplest plan is to take a typical hirsel unit and note the main happenings on it in the round of the year—and starting our survey in November. But first let us have a few definitions and explanations that will help in getting a grip.

A *hirsel* is that particular section of the farm and the sheep on it which it is the primary duty of one shepherd to look after. Sometimes it is a " double " hirsel, in which case the senior shepherd will have an assistant. Other varieties are denoted by their distinguishing prefix of " ewe," " eild " (or yeld) or " mixed."

A ewe hirsel is one on which only breeding ewes (" stock " ewes) and their lambs are kept.

A yeld hirsel carries, of the breeding stock, only sheep of younger ages and in particular the one-year-old females (ewe hoggs) and the rising to two-year-old females (gimmers), neither of which is yet deemed sufficiently matured for mating. On the bigger farms this hirsel usually carries the young females of several ewe hirsels from the time they come home in spring from wintering at a low-ground farm perhaps a hundred miles away until, as young ewes they are returned to their native hirsels to take up the serious business of their lives. In the majority of Black-face stocks this return to the native hirsel takes place in November, when they are aged roughly a year and a half; but in the case of Cheviot stocks, particularly in Sutherland, the gimmers are not thus promoted until they are two and a half years old; and as the period of gestation with sheep is five months it follows that a Black-face ewe usually has her first lamb when she is two years of age, while in the case of Sutherlandshire Cheviots the ewes are three-year-olds when they drop their first lambs.

It might be as well to note here, too, that in the case of both breeds the *theory* is that no ewe is kept on the hill after she has reached the age of five and a half years. Thus it will be seen that at that age the Black-face ewe can have had only four lambs (barring twins), and when she has reared her fourth she is sold off as a cast ewe to be taken down to a low-ground farm to be crossed, usually with a ram of heavier breed for the production of cross lambs (often twins) for the early market. After that gruelling experience her title is changed to the less honourable one of "milled" ewe. Finally, in a year or two, she is converted into what in choosey days might be regarded as sausage mutton but which to-day would be prized as prime gigot.

In the case of the Sutherland Cheviot ewe, as she is a three-year-old when her first lamb is born and as she, too, is cast at five and a half years, it follows that in the course of her life on the hill she can have only three lambs—again barring twins, which on a hill farm are but a mixed blessing anyway. Her post-hill history is much the same as that of her Black-face sister.

And now to go back to early November for a very sketchy glance at the principal events of the year—for by then all sales of sheep and wool are over for the season. The rams, since September, have been strictly segregated within flawless fences; the ewe lambs have been sent off to wintering, the October dipping (statutory) is over, the ewes have had time to recover from the strain of rearing lambs—and the stage is set for the next round.

We will assume a Black-face mixed hirsel. At this time the stock belonging to the hirsel including lambs away at wintering numbers, say, five hundred. Now if hill sheep did not die of disease or suffer death by violence in one shape or another, the age grouping would be quite simple—there would be:

100	four-and-a-half-year-old ewes	
100	three-and-a-half-year-old ewes	400 stock ewes,
100	two-and-a-half-year-old ewes	on the hirsel
100	one-and-a-half-year-old ewes	
100	half-year-old ewe lambs	at wintering

500

But the causes of death among hill sheep are many. Trembling, braxy, sturdy, pine, liver-rot, drowning in bogs and burns, snow-smoor, falling over precipices, foxes, marauding dogs, Black-backs, Hoodie crows, couping and careering motorists are some of the things that play the very deuce with the mathematics of age-grouping of a hill sheep-stock. Even on the " healthiest " of farms and in the luckiest of years an annual death-rate of 6 per cent. would be considered fortunate. Ten per cent. is much more common, and in some districts more than twice that is not unknown. The comparatively moderate figure of 10 per cent. means a loss by death of the equivalent of the whole of your original stock in ten years: a risk far exceeding that in any other type of Scottish farming. In fact, if our average lamb crop is 70 per cent. and our average annual death-rate only 8 per cent., after selling-off female lambs below standard quality, our age-group structure at November would be approximately:

88 four-and-a-half-year-olds	
95 three-and-a-half-year-olds	
104 two-and-a-half-year-olds	stock ewes 400
113 one-and-a-half-year-olds	
124 half-year-old lambs	at wintering

524

or nothing more than is required to maintain the stock ewes at the four hundred level. And we know many places where the ewe lamb crop is lower and the average death-rate higher. And that is why it is that the theoretical and much desired " casting " of five-and-a-half-year-old ewes is so difficult in practice. Often farmers are faced with the alternative of keeping on their old ewes to maintain their breeding stock or of selling them off and letting their stock diminish. It is a sort of Hobson's choice which usually ends by over-age ewes being retained; and that is apt to set agoing a vicious downward spiral in the number and quality of lambs, and ultimately of ewes, which it is mighty difficult to arrest.

The first active step in the year's round is the putting out of the rams to the ewes—roughly in the proportion of three to one hundred—on a date somewhere in the third or fourth week of November. Towards the end of December the rams are taken in and again segregated or sent to low ground for wintering. In some cases they are allowed to summer on the hill along with the ewes and lambs but again relegated to enforced celibacy in September until required the following November.

In *February* there is a gathering of sheep for the *spring dipping*. This is not one of the statutory dippings, but is now generally favoured because of the immunity it gives to the ewe from irritation by skin parasites and consequent betterment in milk supply during the period April-August when she is rearing her lamb. The spring dipping is nicely timed with a view to maximum destruction of parasites and minimum of risk to in-lamb ewes; and in this connection our Scottish weather can be very trying !

Look out for the first lambs twenty-one weeks from the day the rams were put out in November. That will be just *about the same day of the month of April*. From then on for a month, for the shepherd and his specially hired " lamber " assistant, there is hardly any sleep at all. From dawn to dusk, and often through the darkness, their job is to keep watch and ward over their four hundred ewes scattered over a hill range of perhaps two or three thousand acres and now, in the throes of birth-giving, exposed not merely to the normal physical risks and mischances associated with that function, but to the horrible attacks of ruthless Black-backs and Hoodies, scouting overhead to spot the mother in labour, and then sitting on adjacent rocks in fierce mutual jealousy, waiting for the moment the lamb is born to pick from their sockets eyes that have scarcely seen the light of day while the mother is still too weak to protect her baby. Those ghoulish creatures know from experience that their best opportunity is before that man with his dog—and maybe a gun!—comes along. So they come while it is still dark and wait for the first peep of day. Well does the shepherd know that, and he comes early too. But his hill is wide and his pace is relatively slow. He cannot be in half a dozen places at the same time. A few minutes halt to help a ewe in distress, or to give a drop of warm milk to a weakly lamb so that it may get strength to seek its natural source of sustenance, may result in tragedy on the other side of the ridge only a hundred yards away. . . .

And the red fox! that can break the neck of a well-grown lamb and carry it off regardless of mother's pathetically futile fury. . . . And if, from a hundred ewes, sixty to eighty lambs may seem a poor crop, having regard to the nature and variety of difficulties by which he is beset, even that measure of success is no mean achievement.

Truly the hill shepherd's is a job that demands all of a man's loyalty and effort and courage and skill; and truly with these virtues our Scottish hill shepherd is richly endowed. Those who imagine the life of a hill shepherd as a romantic strolling over sunny uplands with spy-glass, collie and crook should see him on a night in February when, from a day that gave no warning, there bursts one of those swirling, blinding, choking, terrifying snowstorms which from time to time cause such havoc in our moorland flocks.

His heft of ewes on the far slope at Alltdearg (some three miles across the moor) so seemingly safe when he saw them but a few hours ago, will be driven helplessly towards that deathtrap of a burn! Never a hesitation as to what must be done—and done instantly. On go the old coat and leggings; the warm woollen gravat is wound round neck and ears; the crook is grasped from its corner; a " Come on, Roy! Bess! " to the dogs; a " Don't expect me till I come " to the wife, and a very gallant trio, without fuss or fear, go forth into that awful night to battle along the trackless treacherous moor with but one thought in mind—to save the ewes from being smothered or drowned at Alltdearg. Yes—not a few shepherds have given their lives that way.

Towards the end of May or early in June there is a big gather for the " marking " of the lambs. All male (wedder) lambs (with the exception of a few specially selected to serve as future rams) are castrated, and the tails of both sexes are docked, *i.e.*, shortened by a few inches. All lambs are also marked (buisted) by having the distinguishing mark of its farm and hirsel tar-stamped on the wool over the appropriate part of the body. Sometimes, too, the female lambs get " ear-marked " to the farm and age-marked as well; but often this distinction is deferred until all inferior and any surplus ewe lambs have been sold off.

Later in June there is a gathering-in of eild sheep for *clipping*.

In July the milk-ewes are clipped. One of the most important events of the year, and, as most of the shearing is done in the open, much at the mercy of the weather; for not even a fleece that is but slightly damp dare be rolled or packed. For catchers, clippers, buisters and packers it's a hot, hard job, which in other days was marvellously lightened by a generous libation of spirituous liquors that inspired tales of old experts and much competition. It's grand to see two experts who happen each to get a sheep from a catcher at the same moment pretending not to notice, but each striving to be the first to snip that last tassel from the tail, and so entitled, a fraction of a second before his neighbour, to get in a stentorian " BUIST ! " to the boy in charge of the boiling tar and buisting irons. And woe betide that youth if he is slow to respond ! By the way, it will save a lot of trouble later if at clipping the five-year-old ewes due for casting in the autumn are specially marked with a " pop " of tar.

As for the ewes and lambs, it is a time of baaing and bleating by day and by night. When at last the penned-up lambs are released to find their newly-shorn mothers the row is beyond belief. There is sometimes the odd lamb or two which refuses to believe that that bleached bleating monstrosity can be mother; but on the whole it is marvellous how quickly and completely the process of mothering is satisfactorily adjusted.

Not so many years ago the getting away of the wool from outlying hirsels and farms was a matter of considerable difficulty. Often it was a case of carrying only a couple at a time of those monstrous wool bags over the moor by pony-back or cart to the junction with a road, from where, in loads of half a dozen bags, it would be carted to the nearest railway station or pier, perhaps forty miles away. Now, with the aid of jeep, caterpillar and motor lorry the annual problem of getting away the wool is a thing of the past.

August, September and October are strenuous months with a continuous succession and variety of jobs. Within this period are due the two statutory dippings—one in August and the other in October—and in parts of the country where autumn hill mists are frequent a " clean gather " for the dippings is often impossible—with consequent irritating hold-ups.

From early August to late September—according to district and custom—come the speaning of the lambs, the expert sorting of the wedder lambs into " top," " mid " and " shott " classes for presentation at the sales, then driving of the lots to the various sale centres—sometimes so far distant as to necessitate an " on drove " period of several days.

Towards the end of September and throughout October the selling of the cast ewes goes on. The ewes, before leaving for the sales, undergo a process of " dressing "— an art in which some shepherds have a skill equal to that required for the achievement of a modern lady's coiffeur.

So, through storm and sunshine and the vicissitudes of the year, to the sales. And what an absorbing climax is this harvest of the hills! In these few weeks will emerge the earning value of their year of strenuous toil; for in that time they will know the value of their wool; and every ewe and lamb and other beast surplus to requirements for the maintenance of the flock will come under the hammer. In respect of all of them the owner will experience that poignant moment which, with a final " Going! Going! Gone! " and a bang of the auctioneer's book, transfers the ownership to another.

Och! it has its ups and downs—mostly downs, according to themselves. But it has its compensations. In truth it's a man's life, and be times good or bad they wouldn't have any other.

CHAPTER XVI

Valuations—An Old Ewe—A Long Lunch

ON many hill farms the sheep-stock is "bound to the ground." None but the annual quota of lambs and cast ewes and rams may be sold off the place. An outgoing tenant is bound by the terms of his lease to deliver over the breeding stock in regular ages to the incoming tenant (or, failing such, to the landlord) so that the advantages of better health and strongly developed homing instinct of a home-bred stock may not be lost to the farm. The method of determining the values is also ruled by the terms of the lease. It may be at "fixed prices"; it may be on a "market-value" basis; or it may be on a full "acclimatisation value" basis—which, prior to recent restrictive statutory enactments, afforded considerable scope for imaginative effort on the part of the experts. Quite recently there has died out an interesting custom which from time immemorial dictated the terms of the award in a sheep-stock valuation. That was the custom of valuing the sheep not at so much *per head* but at so much per *clad score* (a clad score being twenty-one); the proportion of shotts (inferior sheep) in the lot was stated per score (twenty) and fell to be taken over at one-third less than the price stated. Leaving out rams (which would be valued individually or in age groups) a typical award would run thus :

    1057 Ewes and lambs at £57. 10s. per clad score;
        shotts $2\frac{1}{4}$ per score at $\frac{1}{3}$ less.

    122 Yeld ewes at £45 per clad score;
        shotts $1\frac{1}{2}$ per score at $\frac{1}{3}$ less.

    317 Gimmers at £47. 10s. per clad score;
        shotts $1\frac{3}{4}$ per score at $\frac{1}{3}$ less.

    325 Ewe hoggs at £35 per clad score;
        shotts $1\frac{3}{4}$ per score at $\frac{1}{3}$ less.

To arrive at the correct total from an award in such terms was a first-class exercise in arithmetic. Often it was beyond the prowess of both outgoing and incoming tenant. Even with the help of their legal agents the best that could be achieved sometimes was agreement to split the difference between their respective totals that represented hours of laborious calculations. It was the late William MacLennan, for many years factor for Lord Zetland, who about forty years ago first made such calculations easy by the tables in his ready reckoner, *The Flockmaster's Companion*. To arrive at the sum payable in the case of the award quoted above all you had to do was to multiply the total number of sheep in each class by the appropriate figure.

				£	s.	d.
For Ewes and lambs it is	$1057 \times £2 \cdot 635416 =$			£2785	12	8
,, Yeld ewes	,, ,,	$122 \times £2 \cdot 089285 =$		254	17	10
,, Gimmers	,, ,,	$317 \times £2 \cdot 214781 =$		702	1	8½
,, Ewe hoggs	,, ,,	$325 \times £1 \cdot 618055 =$		525	17	4
				£4268	9	6½

William did not visualise any figure above £70 per clad score for ewes and lambs. In 1920-21 and again recently ewes and lambs were going at over £200 per clad score and we had to juggle with the tables.

No wonder that old-time hill farmers sometimes animadvert on present-day nursery-maid methods: of laws that will not allow of men standing on their own feet, and must always be guiding them from chair to chair, so that their lives are robbed of adventure and romance! For them a sheep-stock valuation was a day to be enjoyed and remembered. To it would gather farmers from all over the county, and some from beyond. The neighbouring ones brought their shepherds to give a hand to ensure that every sheep in its class was properly shown to the valuators. Usually there were two of these—one representing the interests of the outgoing tenant and the other of the incoming. There was an oversman in case of non-agreement ; and, as each valuator was all out for his own side, non-agreement was frequent, and the oversman was the person who really mattered. This highly important person was " mutually chosen " by the parties to the valuation. Not infrequently it took many months of mutual and highly diverting sparring for position before the choice could be announced. When no agreement could be arrived at, the appointment of the oversman was remitted to the Sheriff of the county. But the knowledge that in the end they would almost certainly have to submit to the oversman in no wise damped the valuators' ardour in promoting the interests of their respective clients, and their ingenuity and resource in that direction was always a thing to marvel at. In a case where the incoming tenant's expert gives it as his emphatic opinion " before God and with a good conscience " that the gimmers would be dear at £4 apiece, and the expert for the outgoing, under similar solemn guidance and restraint, is equally emphatic that they would be cheap at £6, there is obviously considerable scope for persuasive argument. Variety in technique was infinite. There might be audibly expressed horror at the other's awful position *vis-à-vis* his Creator ; or it might be a whispered (but just audible) concern that neighbours should never be allowed to know the sort of fool he is making of himself in suggesting so absurd a price.

Nor is partisanship always strictly confined to the valuators. If one can do a good turn by a remark which happens to reach the valuator's ears, but does not appear to be made with that end in view at all, should one refrain from making it?

One old worthy I knew was a master of that sort of

innocent soliloquy. On this day the valuator with the incoming tenant's interest at heart had suggested that amongst the ewes presented for valuation was a number of over-age animals whose presence seriously detracted from the value of the lot—an outrageous suggestion strongly repudiated by the outgoing tenant's man. There followed a hot exchange of contradictory assertions which promised to end in a laborious inspection of lug-marks in search of truth. It was just then that old Angus (who was friendly disposed towards the incoming tenant but appeared not to have taken the slightest interest in the point at issue) took advantage of a momentary lull in the brawl. He was looking at a venerable ewe which had lain on a nearby hillock and, regardless of all the fuss, was placidly chewing her cud. In a voice charged with sentimental emotion Angus addressed the ewe:

" *A ghalad! Tha thu 'n sin air an tomain cnamh do chìre direach mar a bha thu 'nuair bha mi so seachd bliadhna bho 'n diugh!* " (" My dear! There you are on the hillock, chewing your cud just as you were when I was here seven years ago to-day! ")

Generous hospitality was a feature of old-time sheep-stock valuations—in the dispensing of which the wives of farmers and sometimes of shepherds came in for a strenuous time. On one such occasion I was greatly impressed by the efficiency of the managing shepherd's wife (whom I had not previously met) who, with the assistance of one neighbour and a lassie in her teens, cooked and served in the one day 22 breakfasts, 46 lunches and 34 high teas. She was a pleasant, good-looking woman, and though very stout could have given points to some professional waiters I have known.

The valuation was on a Wednesday. On the following Saturday I called again at the shepherd's place to take delivery of some " stragglers " that had come in since the valuation. The door was open, but I got no response to a knock. I went round to the back to see if there was anyone about the byre or barn. I heard the sound of milking. There in the byre was a stranger milking a cow. She was a tall slim girl and gave a pleasant greeting as she continued at her task.

I explained that I had called to see the shepherd but found nobody in the house. Could she tell me where the shepherd or his wife was to be found?

She looked somewhat puzzled, and then really surprised me by saying, " But I am the shepherd's wife ! "

" I beg your pardon ! " I said, " I am really very sorry ! But I thought it was the shepherd's wife who looked after us all so well on the day of the valuation ! "

" Well," said she, " and so it was ! "

" But no ! no ! " I protested, " I mean the big stout woman who was in charge."

" Well," she insisted, " the big stout woman was me ! "

" But bless me ! " I bleated, fair puzzled, " I just do not understand. I . . . ? "

" Oh ! I see ! " she said with a grin. " But if you go to the kitchen till I finish this cow, and see that the baby in the cradle is all right, perhaps you will begin to understand."

I went to the kitchen. There in the cradle I found an exceptionally healthy specimen of a baby boy. He had been born on the morning of the day after the valuation; he was not two days old and his mother was in the byre blithely milking the cow.

But the high-water mark in hospitality at a sheep-stock valuation in my experience was reached that time we sat down to a lunch that started at 1 P.M. and didn't really finish till 4 A.M. next day. True, many of the original starters didn't stay the course: there were several casualties and departures in the late afternoon and there

were somewhat hazy intervals here and there when it
could not be claimed that all the survivors were *eating*
at the tables. But always, up till 10 P.M., a dozen or
two could be relied on to carry on with the knives and
forks while the others kept up the general hilarity to
the best of their ability; which latter was of no mean
order.

There followed a pretty tough session till midnight, by
which time all but twenty of the original starters weren't
there. At 3.30 A.M. the remaining eight of us found
ourselves seated at one table feeling quite peckish and
putting in a hearty finish to the long lunch. Included in
the party were A and B who, though bosom friends of
many years, had recently fallen out over something and
hadn't spoken to each other for months. Not even the
extreme cordiality which characterised the day's proceedings had broken down the barriers—a state of affairs
which became all the more delicate in so small a company.
Tension was relieved, though, when we observed that A,
with head sunk on chest, had presumably fallen sound
asleep.

At this stage B got to his feet and begged to announce
to the assembled company that before parting on this so
auspicious occasion he felt it incumbent on himself to
propose a toast: the toast of " The Arbiter." The
proposal met with a hearty approval that gave no hint
of the fact that the arbiter had already in the course of
the evening been toasted at least a dozen times. We
hear—heared! with virginal zest.

In a model of a speech of some six minutes duration,
B extolled the virtues of the arbiter's parents, his boy-
hood, youth and manhood, and touched on his crowning
glory as an arbiter.

All bar A, who was apparently still sound asleep, did full
justice to the occasion and in chorus shouted " Arbiter !

Arbiter! Arbiter!" and resumed our seats. That is, all but B, who remained upright and, as soon appeared, was of the opinion he had got up to say something. Then it came to him. He begged to announce to the assembled company that, before parting on this so auspicious occasion, he felt it incumbent on himself to propose a toast: the toast of "The Arbiter"! And word for word like a gramophone record he reproduced the model speech.

Though some of us were somewhat surprised we all got up as best we could and again gave cordial reception to the toast. A was still asleep.

Still B remained on his feet, deep in mental struggle, and—to the surprise of all of us this time—again submitted the toast of "The Arbiter."

And again we responded.

But when B for the fourth time began to beg to announce to the assembled company, etc. . . . the spell under which we had laboured for nearly twenty minutes was suddenly broken. The sleeping A, with the aid of a firm grip on the underpart of the table, managed to raise his bottom about six inches from the chair. Through half-closed eyes he peered round the table.

"Gentlemen," he said, "as shelf appoined shairman of shis meeting I beg ta nounsh to shembled cupney that speshes be of shree minitsh shurashion—AN NO REPETI-SHUNS!"

During this surprising announcement B stood gazing malevolently at the interrupter. Now in concentrated anger he addresses the enemy.

"Sir, do you mean to insinuate that I am *boring* the company?"

A again raised his bottom off the chair, glowered vaguely in the direction of B, said, "I jew," sat down and went off to sleep.

The electrical atmosphere could be cleared only by a diversion; so we all struggled to our feet and in honour of the arbiter, sang " He's a jolly good fellow " about ten times over; followed up with Auld Lang Syne, and beat a hurried retreat while the going was still good.

CHAPTER XVII

Shetland—Self-help—Seafaring Breed

THE official name now is Zetland, but like most people I feel more at home with Shetland. Here is a county of more than a hundred islands, of which over twenty are inhabited. Foula, the island of film fame, stands sentinel some thirty miles out to the west of the mainland; and Fair Isle, some twenty-five miles south-west of Sumburgh Head, is a sort of half-way house to Orkney.

From Sumburgh Head in the south, to Muckle Flugga in the north—the most northerly land (or rather rock) in Britain—is some seventy miles.

A visit to the Muckle Flugga is something to be remembered. The day we went the weather was so fine that our boatman decided to take us through a tunnel opening in a cliff. At high tide or in a heavy swell it is impossible to get a boat through this hole in the wall of rock. Even on that good day there was a dreadful moment when it seemed that the gentle swell would result in our being crushed like an egg-shell against the roof of the tunnel. We were heartily glad to get safely through; but when we got to the base of the Muckle Flugga at the landing place from which an incredible number of steps cut in the rock-face lead to the lighthouse at the top, it was only fear of losing face that goaded us into making that fearsome ascent. The indescribably impressive view from the top temporarily dispelled even our dread of the down-coming; and of course we got from the lighthouse-keeper the sort of welcome which only lighthouse-keepers can give.

Shetland is so deeply indented by " voes " (firths) that any figure of breadth from east to west would have little meaning; enough to say that although at its widest it is 22 miles broad, you cannot stand on a spot in Shetland that is three miles from the sea.

Roughly up the middle of the long streak which forms the mainland there is a back-bone of hills rising from 500 to 900 feet and culminating in Ronas Hill, which is nearly 1,500 feet and the highest point in the county.

The total land area is 352,000 acres; but of this only 14,000 acres or so is cropping land. The great bulk of the remainder is common pasture—or " scattald " to give it its local name. A feature which at once attracts the notice of a stranger is the comparatively large area of cabbages. The Shetlander sets great value on his cabbages as a winter feed for stock. The favourite variety is of a purplish colour and peculiar to these islands. Cabbage seed is preserved each year and sown for safety in " plantiecruives." The plantiecruive is a small nursery out on the scattald, with high walls to protect the young plants from the devastating winds, and from the depreda- tion of even the most enterprising of sheep—which is saying a good deal in Shetland !—until transplanted in garden land and well-enclosed paddocks near the house. Despite disadvantages of soil and climate the standard of agriculture has been markedly raised in recent years.

Shetland is a county of small-holdings. Out of a total of nearly 4,000 agricultural subjects over 3,000 are under the 50-acre standard (disregarding share in scattald), and of these 3,000 more than half do not exceed five acres. The rights of participation in the scattald grazing is a subject so complicated as to be almost incomprehensible to an outsider, but to the participants themselves it seems simple enough. That is not to say they are always of one mind about it—as the Scottish Land Court, whose unenviable duty sometimes is to settle local differ- ences of opinion on the matter, very well know !

Everybody knows that Shetland has a pony of its own;

also that it has its own miniature collie dog. But not so many know that Shetland has also got its own breed of cattle and sheep.

The Shetland pony is too well known to require description: it should be emphasised, though, that the sleek, well-groomed, well-mannered specimens familiar at Lowland shows bear but little resemblance to the shaggy, wild-eyed creatures which roam in droves over their native scattald.

Ponies used to be exported in considerable numbers. They made ideal pets for children of the well-to-do, but the main demand for them was as pit-ponies for hauling coal from the working face to the elevators at the pit shaft. Soon after the Great War, following the installation of electric power in the pits, the demand for them became so poor that few were exported. The result was an embarrassing increase in their numbers at home. They ate up the sheep's pasture to such an alarming and lossful extent that scores of them had to be shot and buried. In one case I had to do with, where over fifty ponies had to be cleared off the ground, as an alternative to shooting (which I couldn't bring myself to do) I had them sent for sale at Aberdeen; but to meet all charges for freight, keep and commission I had to pay £15 in excess of the total sum realised from the sale! In recent years the demand for Shetland ponies has revived, and at the moment they are fetching good prices.

The Shetland cow is a sort of Shorthorn in miniature, very hardy, a good milker and said to be free of tuberculosis. With this reputation she is in considerable demand as a " family " cow both in and outwith Shetland.

In recent years there has been a good deal of crossing of the native sheep with the Cheviot, Black-face and other heavier breeds, but the real Shetland sheep is a dainty creature not so very much larger than an outsize Mid-

9

lothian brown hare. The infallible mark of the breed is a short, *bare* tail. Colours are white, black, black and white, and a warm brown or " moorit." The wool, which is very fine, is not shorn but *plucked* off the body (" rooing"). This is the wool which is the basis of the world-famous Shetland hosiery industry.

The artistic skill and speed displayed by the women in designing and knitting have got to be seen to be believed. Shawls and garments of intricate design and of beautifully blended colours are made " straight out of their heads." Nor does the adage about the wisdom of doing only one thing at a time hold much meaning for these wonderful women of Shetland, who can simultaneously carry a creel of peats, drive a cow, enjoy an animated conversation with a neighbour similarly employed and knit one of these garments, all with amazing proficiency.

Minerals. Cromate and copper ore are known to exist in various places, particularly in the island of Unst, and to a limited extent the mines have been worked at different times in the past. In any national scheme of rural regeneration it is conceivable that these deposits may assume local importance.

Herring Fishing. After agriculture—and some might dispute the " after "—herring fishing is the great industry in Shetland. With the advent of the steam drifter in place of the old sailing boat the fishing industry has, during the past thirty years, centred mainly in Lerwick, to which English and West Coast boats and " crews " of lassies repair annually at the opening of the " season " in that spirit of high hope and adventure so characteristic of all engaged in this tantalising but occasionally very remunerative calling.

To the extent that the general circumstances of their lives are similar, the Shetlander and the man of the

Western Isles are very much alike. Insularity makes of each a good boatman and skilful fisherman; and he is weather-wise and independent in outlook. But certain characteristics attributable to racial differences are noticeable. When the Celt is impulsive and maybe dangerously imaginative, the Scandinavian is a philosopher in close touch with realities. Seldom does a Celt in search of a small-holding bother to reconcile his demand with his capital resources. With not a penny to bless him he will airily inscribe the figure 50 in the blank on the official form when he is invited to state the acreage of the holding he is applying for. That it takes around £500 to fully stock and equip a fifty-acre holding daunts your penniless Highlander not a whit, and he is indignant when a friendly but unfortunate official points out the snags. In marked contrast the Shetlander carefully counts the cost and inserts an acreage figure in strict accordance with his financial capacity; and if he is offered land in excess of that acreage he politely but firmly refuses to accept.

I shall probably get into hot water over this next bit, for, as a Celt, I can think of no epithet more likely to arouse hot resentment, when applied to my kinsmen, than that of " beggar." Yet the fact is that, in the course of the past fifty years, in his relationship with government departments and local authorities the Celt has acquired a skill in alms-collecting that amounts to genius. Singly and collectively, by political pressure, by telling the tale of woe with a skill worthy of the *seanachaidh*, the Highlander has contrived to ensure a considerable flow in his direction of the fluid that comes from such old milk-cows. Time and again he has successfully persisted in his claim to have a new road or path or pier. Seasons of potato-blight or bad harvests skilfully publicised have resulted in supplies of seed-potatoes and oats the following spring. He is still at it and likely to continue. Nor do I suggest that he has got anything in excess of his value to the nation in peace and war. I am merely concerned to show an interesting difference between Highlander and Shetlander.

The Shetlander suffers adverse circumstances in silence. Seldom does he make public moan. I well remember a case where the crofters in a Shetland township applied to the Department of Agriculture for enlargement of holdings. On local investigation I found that the land applied for was on the far side of a heather-clad moor and nearly a mile distant from the existing crofts; and there was no road across the moor. I had to point out to the applicants that, even if they got the land and grew crops on it they would not be able to get the crops home for want of a road—and that it was doubtful if the Department would regard the cost of a road as justifiable in this particular case. The applicants appreciated the point and said they would write me when they had further considered their problem. Six months later I had a letter from their secretary. Could I come to see them soon? *They had constructed a road across the moor and would be glad if the scheme for enlarging their crofts could now be proceeded with!* Of course I went—and found a well-constructed road from the crofts to the land they wanted. It transpired that, following on my previous visit, they resolved to overcome the obstacle by making a road for themselves; so they appointed as foreman one of themselves who had some skill in road work. Each of the others contributed a share of the labour necessary to complete the road—and there it was! Only in Shetland did I ever meet so amazing a capacity for self-help.

During the war a Secretary of State for Scotland paid a visit to Shetland. One of the things he particularly wished to see was one of those primitive little meal-mills, whose circular grinding-stone is made to revolve by the flow of water from a burn being directed towards its flanged spindle. The Agricultural College representative took us to see one. It was in excellent condition and hard at work grinding bere into meal. The Secretary of State was much impressed by the ingenuity and efficiency of the mill, and astonished to learn that its every part had been made and put together by the crofter to whom it belonged and his father.

The crofter offered to show us the kiln where he dried the grain before milling. To get to the kiln we had to go through an exceptionally well-constructed barn. The Secretary supposed that this was the work of a professional builder?

" Weel, as a matter of fact, no: it was himself who had built the barn too " ! was the modest claim.

I noticed in the barn a neatly finished fanner—but not of any " make " known to me.

" Did you make this too? " I inquired.

" Oh weel, yes: he had made that too—in his spare time one winter."

The kiln was of the " bellied-cone " type, built of stone, about ten feet high at the apex and perfect in its proportions and symmetry. Even I did not think any amateur could have built so perfect a structure—and said as much. But he had !

" But how on earth did you get the outbulges and the inward curves so faultless? " I wondered.

" Oh weel, I hed to think oot that one weel before I started. First I cleared the foundation. Then I fixed a peg in the centre and with a piece of string attached to it I drew a circle of the size I wanted. Then I took oot the peg and put a ten-foot pole standing on the same spot, and plumbed it there with light wood-stays. Then I drew on a piece of paper (to scale) a plan of the kiln I wanted, with its sides bulging out from the centre and then curving in to converge truly at the apex. Then I cut a number of strings of the different lengths required to give me my right radius from the centre pole at every half foot of height—and man! it cam oot fine!"

After this it came as no surprise that the very substantial and well finished dwelling-house, from foundation to roof-ridging, had been planned and executed by this master craftsman, who had never learned any trade but coopering. But indeed the Secretary was moved to genuine admiration, and in the course of conversation was distressed to learn that our host was beginning to feel the work of the place too much for one of his years. Worse still, of his two sons, the one who used to help him was already in the navy and the other one who was in a bank and helped him at week-ends was due to join the army next week. It was certainly a hard case and the Secretary, who was very human and kind of heart, had a whispered conversation with the senior departmental official who was present. The senior official, while equally sympathetic, very rightly pointed out the danger of making any promises which might not be fulfillable. So the Secretary was very guarded in expressing to the old man the hope that something might be done; he would see; he would do his best; but he could not promise. . . .

Not till then did our host suspect what had been the subject of the whispered conversation.

"Are you telling me, sir, that you may be able to do something to keep my boy at home?" he asked.

Well, the Secretary would like to—he would try; but of course he couldn't promise.

The old man was wistfully silent for a minute, then: "Well, sir, that is very kind of you, and I expect it would take a load off his mother's heart—although I'm not sure that she would like it either. But you see, sir, the last time he was with us we could see he was unhappy at not being away at the war with the rest of them. And we don't want him to be unhappy—and I hope you will not misunderstand or think me ungrateful, but we would raither you did not do anything about it but just let things be. But thank you very much for your kindness."

Seafaring is in the Shetlander's blood. The proportion of men from these islands who earn their livelihood by going down to the sea in ships (in ways more peaceful than those of their viking forebears!) is very great. In Shetland you can meet hundreds of men who are as familiar with Sydney harbour and Magellan's Strait as they are with Lerwick and Scalloway; quiet, keen-eyed, clear-headed, decent men worthily upholding in every quarter of the globe the best traditions of their breed. But their roots are deep in Shetland whither they repair between voyages to recuperate on the land; and later to seek refuge and peace in the evening of life.

CHAPTER XVIII

Usgar* : Being Red-letter Days in the Life of a Highland Cow

(This chapter is for bairns only—of all ages)

SHE was born out on the machair of a township in the Hebrides. It was a bonnie April morning that set the larks acarolling in the sun despite a remnant of winter's chill in the air.

She wasn't quite yellow, nor yet quite brown, but yon in-between colour which denotes a hardy constitution. And she was as curly as a toy teddy bear; indeed, that was what she looked like lying in the shelter of the tuft of sea-bent.

Her mother (Annag), not content with the thorough cleansing she had already given her baby daughter, was still giving a lick here and there, and softly moaning an invitation to be up and doing at a first meal from an udder that ached with its amplitude of rich warm milk. Suddenly mother sensed approaching danger and whipped round on the defensive ! . . . But it was only her mistress, Kirsty, coming to see if the expected calf had yet arrived. A glance at the little stranger and Kirsty knew that her wish of many years was at last satisfied.

" *M'usgair bheag!* " (" My precious little jewel ! ") cried Kirsty, and her gently caressing the curly coat while Annag looked on with a fondly-fatuous expression of eye that was comical in the extreme. Now the reason for Kirsty's great joy was this:

Annag's great-great-great-grandmother Morag had come to the croft as a wedding gift to Kirsty's husband's father from *his* father. That was a long time ago, but always since then there had been on the place a descendant of

* Sound the u *not* as in *but* but as in *puss* ; and the word as a whole sounds *usscar.*

136

the wedding-gift cow. But it had looked as if Annag would be the last of her line. For years Kirsty had hoped that Annag would produce a daughter. But no! year after year it was a great big son she presented to Kirsty; and now, after so many disappointments, there was Annag's little daughter that would one day take up the succession as the favourite cow on the croft. No wonder that Kirsty called this calf her precious little jewel! That evening, her tummy well filled with milk, wee Usgar lay beside her mother on the machair looking far out to sea, where a great golden ball was sinking slowly out of sight and sending up into the sky a succession of resplendent yellows and pinks and reds and purples that together on this first day of her life evoked in Usgar a vague bovine bliss.

. . . .

In describing the first day of Usgar's life I purposely made no mention of the less pleasant subject of death; but the fact is that Kirsty's man Donald had died some years before Usgar was born. He, too, had been hoping that Annag would some day have a heifer calf; and that was another reason for Kirsty's joy at sight of Usgar. Meantime her son Donald had joined the Cameron Highlanders and was away at the war, while the widow was doing her best to carry on the croft with the help of neighbours.

There came a day in late autumn that brought to little Usgar the first great unhappiness of her life. The previous day there had been a blood-red sky as the sun went down. Angus, the herd "Aonghas a' bhuachaille" prophesied to Kirsty that this foretold an early frost. Sure enough that very night there was a sharp frost and a million stars in a steel-blue sky. The ground hardened. Ice came on the pools. The calves' skins felt creepy with the cold. By morning they were feeling pretty miserable. But far, far worse was yet to come! When Aonghas came along that morning Kirsty came too, and Hector and Calum Saighdear and three or four dogs. Why all this? But when the people and the dogs tried to separate them from their mothers the youngsters sensed that something unusual and unpleasant was afoot.

Truth to tell, for some time past they had not been keeping so very close to their mothers because, with the browning grass, milk was getting scarce; and they took a mischievous pride in keeping far away from the cows, who would get alarmed and start calling at them to come back. But there was a mighty difference between calves voluntarily separating themselves from their mothers and being forcibly driven from them! For a while they defied every effort in that direction, but in the end, with the help of hard sticks and biting dogs, the people managed to turn back the calves while their mothers were driven through a gate and far away out of sight.

Little did the youngsters think that never again would they taste a drop of their mother's milk. Surely before long they would be allowed to join their mothers again! But hour after hour passed and they got really alarmed. Not till then did they realise how much their mothers meant to them. They started a chorus of heart-broken bellowing that their mothers could have heard in St Kilda. Anyhow, they heard it where they were, for they set up a bellowing too; and so it continued through that awful day of black misery and thirst. At last thirst compelled them to sip the ice-cold water, which gave them a toothache and pains in the tummy. By night they were too tired and miserable even to bellow. For them the end of the world had come as they lay on the cold frosty ground to pass the most wretched night of their lives.

But after a few miserable days they were still alive— and began to take an interest in life again. So much so, that when one morning Aonghas opened the gate and drove them over to where their mothers were they seemed somewhat ashamed of all the noise they had made about the separation. They merely sniffed their mothers when they met—all but Calum Beag who was calf enough to try for a sip at the old source—and got kicked in the face for his impudence! Calum was deeply offended, but the rest of them with tails in air danced for joy at his discomfiture, and felt quite grown-up and self-reliant.

· · · · · · · · · · ·

By the time she was eighteen months old, Usgar had grown into a fine stirk and was already showing a pair of horns of great promise. Soon she had learned that if Kirsty had a kind heart she had also a quick temper and a hazel switch with which to beat one sorely!

But how can a young creature full of life always be minding p's and q's even if forgetting them may bring a spot of trouble? Anyway, Usgar and her friends got themselves into a whole peck of troubles this day. They had been grazing slowly over the machair from one side to another, with Aonghas a' Bhuachaille keeping an eye to see that they didn't get into mischief. But old Aonghas loved an afternoon nap, and that sometimes gave them the chance of a stolen bite. This day, as they were nearing the dyke that separated the machair from the arable land and feeding on the now rather tasteless autumn grass, the band of youngsters suddenly ceased grazing and stuck their noses in the air to sniff the breeze that came from the crofts. Never had so delectable a smell entered their noses! What it came from they could not guess, but that it was from something that would be good to eat there was no doubt at all. It brought slobbering slavers to their mouths!

Soon all the noses were pointing straight at a dark green patch in Kirsty's croft. Well they knew from painful experience that the crofts were forbidden ground. But their buachaille was sound asleep! And there were gaps on the dyke where they could easily get over! With one accord they jumped the dyke and raced for the green patch.

As that was the first time they had seen turnips they did not know how good the bulbs were to eat. But that didn't bother them : the green shaws had a flavour that stirred their hearts to a frenzy of joy. So for a few happy minutes they just pulled up turnip after turnip and chewed off the green tops.

While they were still hard at their feast there came a shriek from Kirsty and her calling loudly for the dog. Roy came racing at them in a most unfriendly way, barking like mad and snapping at their heels. The noise wakened up old Aonghas, who now ran over with *his* dog and belaboured them on the ribs with his big stick. By this time, too, Kirsty herself had arrived to help with her hazel switch, and with some dreadful names she called them in the Gaelic. Usgar, in her terror, turned on the yapping Roy and with her horns tossed him clean over the dyke, so that he began howling too! Kirsty and Aonghas and the dogs and themselves bawling and bellowing and howling together! Never was such a hullabaloo about a few turnips!

Thinking it all over as they lay on the machair that night with sore heels and ribs, Usgar came to the conclusion that if they wanted to escape trouble in future they had better leave turnips alone—and yet! they smelled so good and tasted so divinely! Perhaps it was meant that way? that for things worth having it is worth risking a spot of trouble? Anyhow, they had those glorious few minutes, even if it did upset the old lady and Aonghas and the dogs—*Nyum Nyum!*

Young Donald was now home from the war. Through the lovely green-grass days of spring and summer Usgar saw him and his neighbours hard at work on the land, sowing and planting, and carting the seaware and peats. Why on earth human beings should always be work-work-working away must be difficult for a cow to understand; but surely it must give them no little satisfaction to see men and women spend most of their days in preparing food for them, so that they may lie in the sun blissfully chewing the cud !

Late in July there came into Usgar's life another of those days which she would long remember. It was the day of the agricultural show. Nearly all the people on the island came to it. That morning Donald had tied a rope round Usgar's horns, brushed her long silken coat with a brush in a way that she half liked and half didn't, then he led her off to the show-ground about five miles away. There they found gathered together the pick of the island's cattle. Usgar was led into the ring by Donald when it came to the time for heifers of her age to be judged—and Donald became the envy of the island that day ! For Usgar, now over three years of age, had developed into a beauty that even in that select company was outstanding. While still retaining the sprightliness and glorious bloom of youth she had acquired some of that stateliness of carriage, that majesty of mien, that was to distinguish her for the rest of her days. Not one moment did the judges hesitate. The first prize red ticket was tied round Usgar's horns; and before the show was over there was an assortment of championship tickets with it, dangling over her nose. Both for Kirsty and Donald this was indeed a memorable day.

Then a thing so dreadful happened that it hurts to tell of it. Ever since he returned from the war Donald had been moody and nervous and not like his old self at all; more than once he had taken more drink than was good for him. This hurt Kirsty to the heart, but she rightly put it down to the upset of the war, and hoped and prayed that some day her son would grow into his old reliable self again. Unfortunately, though, he had not yet regained his serenity and stability; and his outstanding success at the show was too much for him: along with several friends he had made a merry night of it. He was never quite sure of what had happened, but was horrified next morning when a drover came to take Usgar away with some other beasts he had bought! So *that* explained the large sum of money Donald had found in his purse! He had sold Usgar! Usgar that was the pride of his mother's heart—and indeed of his own!

So their day of triumph was followed by a day of grief too deep even to be spoken about. Usgar and the others were driven off to the pier, and that same evening hoisted in a sling to a most alarming height and then dumped down in the bowels of a ship to be carried far away, and finally forced into the sea to swim to the rough, rocky, uninhabited island which was to be Usgar's home for seven years.

· · · · · · · · · ·

After swimming to land on their new island home, Usgar and her friends walked across the little sandy bay and scrambled up a dangerous path through rocks in search of something to eat. The people who used to live on this island had left some years before Usgar landed there. Only cattle and sheep lived there now, and it might be months before a man came to see how they were doing or to shear the sheep or take away some of them to the sales.

While the newcomers were doing their best to satisfy their hunger by eating the short but sweet grass they found above the rocks, what should move into sight, not a hundred yards away, but a number of Highland cows that had been there for years? These old-timers grew quite excited on seeing the strangers. Soon they decided that the strangers had no right to be on their grazing. Two or three of the biggest and wildest looking, with noses to the ground and up-staring eyes, moved towards the newcomers bellowing an awesome challenge. No wonder if most of the tired and still hungry youngsters were terrified and made off for the hills. But not Usgar. For in cattle, as in people, blood tells, and in Usgar's veins ran the blood of that famous sire of old, Tormaid Buidhe of Baile Raonuill. She was young and would probably get hurt by this infuriated and full-grown cow, but she could not run away like one base-born. So she lowered her head to the challenge.

Surprised and further angered by such presumption the big cow, who was clearly the Queen of the Fold, rushed forward to heave Usgar over the almost precipitous face of the rock. But Usgar, well knowing she would have no chance in a head-on charge with a cow nearly twice her weight, flashed round to the side so that in her mad rush the big cow charged straight on—at nothing! Usgar saw her chance—and took it. Before the old cow managed to pull up near the top of the cliff Usgar charged; and what she lacked in weight she made good in youthful agility. Over the rock went her huge adversary, emitting a terrified bellow as she fell.

The old cow was not killed—as she might well have been; nor did she break a leg. But she was badly bruised and slightly lame for the rest of her life. And from that day on Usgar reigned the undisputed Queen of the Island.

.   .   .   .

Every year to the Scottish Highlands from April till October there is a constant stream of visitors to enjoy the peace and grandeur of our scenery. They come from all over the world, and many of them come year after year. The majority of them keep to the main routes, but always there are some who go searching into all sorts of odd and out-of-the-way places. It was one of this kind who one day landed on the island to which Usgar swam ashore some seven years earlier. He was a wealthy gentleman farmer from England and had with him his fifteen-year-old daughter who was greatly enjoying her first visit to the Hebrides. It was the girl who first caught sight of a number of animals, the like of which she had never seen before—and which indeed gave her quite a fright with their great long horns and shaggy coats. But her father assured her they were just Highland cows and very quiet and docile. The cattle had been longing to see a human being and readily made friends with the strangers. One of the friendliest was a magnificent animal with long silky hair and great level horns that spread wider than the length of the girl's body. This beautiful cow came right up and licked the lassie's hand with a rough but kindly tongue, and the father thought the two of them made a rare picture. In a jiffy he had taken a snapshot of them. As father and daughter were about to set off again in their boat, a man came over the hill and gave them a friendly hail. He turned out to be the owner of the cattle and was paying one of his periodic visits to see how they were doing. Mr Osborne made a complimentary remark about the cattle they had seen, and made special mention of the beautiful big cow that was so friendly.

Mr Stewart agreed they were a fine lot and regretted he must soon sell the big cow, because, although she was by far the best, she had disappointed him in that she had never produced a heifer calf: seven bull calves in a row!

Now Mr Osborne had often thought of starting a

small fold of Highland cattle at his place in England. Here might be his chance—and it was almost certain that a cow which had so many sons would soon have a daughter!

In a few minutes a bargain was struck. Usgar—for Usgar it was—would be shipped next week to Kyle and railed to the south of England. And the clattering and rattling of the train and the awful hunger of that long journey remained in her memory for many a day.

. . . .

Other seven years passed. Donald had long ago settled down into a steady-going man with wife and family. Kirsty was now an old woman, but still hale and hearty. Never one word of reproach had she spoken to Donald about the selling of Usgar. But well he knew how it had hurt her, and many had been his own remorseful moments about that unhappy affair.

Donald had flourished exceedingly on the croft, and when they got news that a favourite niece was to be married in London before leaving for Canada, nothing would do but Donald must go and give away the bride.

At the wedding he met a far-out cousin of whom he had little previous knowledge. But, of course, cousins are cousins. This one was manager on a farm a few hours by train west of London. Donald must go to see him before starting for home.

The cousin never said a word about having Highland cattle on the farm; he wanted to give Donald a real surprise. And he did! There were over a dozen very fine cows and a few younger beasts. As the two men stood in the park to have a right look at the animals, there happened to be grazing quite close to them a cow of magnificent proportions, but obviously well up in years. Moving slowly along as she grazed, this cow got right into Donald's " wind " just at the moment when

Donald expressed his admiration for so grand a cow: " '*ille! nach eile i sin math ged a the i aosda?* " Suddenly the old cow ceased grazing, raised her head and sniffed into the breeze. Then she came slowly towards the men, with her nose still in the wind. They watched her with curiosity. She came right up and sniffed Donald's Harris tweed plus-fours!—and then looked up straight at him.

" Strange! I never saw her do the like of that before," said the cousin in the Gaelic.

" Aye," said Donald, also in the old language, and him fair trembling with excitement and looking closely for certain colourings on the cow's sides till he found what he was looking for. " Aye! it's her right enough! It must be—it is our *Usgar!* " And, as if in confirmation, the old cow was now licking his one hand while he rubbed behind her ears with the other.

Briefly Donald told the story of Usgar to the cousin. He knew she had been taken to the island, but there had lost all trace of her. The cousin told of how she came from the island seven years ago, that she had a heifer calf in her first year on the farm but all bull calves since. She was now in calf again; he was selling her soon but he would try to buy her calf back if it should be a heifer.

" You are selling her this very day," said Donald, " and that to me. And you will never get her calf whatever it is! " And that was how it was settled between them without further ado.

. . . .

So it was that Usgar once again found herself in a railway truck on a long, long journey. But she was neither lonely nor hungry this time, for Donald travelled by the same train and had a word with her whenever there was anything of a wait at a station. He also saw to it that she had plenty to eat and drink till they reached

Oban. And when it came to getting her aboard the steamer for the Outer Isles there was no need for twisting tail or slashing stick. The old cow walked down the tilted gangway in the manner of one knowing where she was going.

Out in the Minch, while the Islands were not yet in sight, Usgar was seen to be strangely excited and kept turning her head towards the side of the ship where a modicum of daylight showed. At the pier she walked briskly ashore. From then on it was Usgar that led the way—and at such a pace that Donald was hard put to it to keep up with her. Before they reached home it was dark. She made straight for the gateway that gave entrance to the machair. Donald let down the rails. Usgar walked in and made for where other cows had gone to rest for the night. Soon she lay beside them, tired indeed, for she had travelled far and was heavy with calf, but so much—so very much—*at home*.

Donald walked over in the darkness to the house. He regaled the household with tales of London and the wedding; but of the extraordinary story of Usgar he did not breathe a word.

. . . .

Next morning Donald was up early. There was promise of a good day: already the sun was breaking through the vapoury mist of an April morning.

" Mother," said Donald to Kirsty, " I would like you to come with me to the machair to see one of the cows."

Kirsty wondered why; but Donald made subtle flattery of her greater wisdom and experience in bovine troubles: he would like her advice. So the two set off.

Kirsty could not help thinking how like this lovely morning was to that morning of long ago when . . . But no: she must not allow her thoughts to dwell on that old sore.

The usual cattle were there and Kirsty wondered which it was that Donald wanted her advice about; they all looked in the best of health.

But Donald led on round the bent-covered sand-dune to the very spot where Usgar had seen the light of day for the first time. And there was a great old cow licking her new-born heifer calf.

And in a jiffy, there was Kirsty with the tears running down the runnels in her wrinkled cheeks, once again fondling a curly coat and saying over and over again " *M' Usgar bheag!* " just as she said it that morning seventeen years ago.

CHAPTER XIX

Lord Leverhulme in Harris

In my book *Highland Journey* where I try to tell something of the local reaction to the late Lord Leverhulme's well-meant effort to introduce an industrial régime in the island of Lewis, I deliberately kept to the main feature of the story for fear of wearying readers with non-essential details. Yet some of the side-happenings were not without humour in themselves, and highly interesting as emphasising the wide and fundamental difference in outlook between the great industrial magnate and the native crofting people.

It might have been assumed that so shrewd a man as Lord Leverhulme, after listening to the amazingly eloquent exposition of the local point of view by a crofter-fisherman, would have sensed the deep-rooted cause of the local opposition to his schemes and made some changes in his plans and policy calculated to get round the difficulty. Certainly, at the time, he seemed thoroughly to appreciate the importance of what had been said. But it soon became apparent that to a man of his experience, a philosophy of life and living so simple as that of the crofters was just incomprehensible: to such a man, the acquisition of money must surely be the dominant motive in all men's lives! True, he did make one astute effort. The idea originated on the night of the dinner at the Castle. In our after-dinner private conclave despite my candidly expressed conviction that, by fighting the people on the question of granting them crofts under the Act he could never hope to get their support to his schemes, he continued to press hard for my support and assistance. Was there any way I could suggest that might help? Anything he could do?

I doubted if there was; but in any case there were in every district natural leaders without whose good-will nothing could be done. At the meeting at the farm that morning he had told them of the grand houses and prosperous circumstances of his employees in Port Sunlight. But in such matters seeing was believing. Perhaps if some of the local leaders could see with their own eyes . . . ?

There was no need to say more. Like shot he was on to the idea.

Who were the leaders? How many of them? Ten? Twenty? Fifty? A hundred? He would have the matter arranged first thing in the morning. . . . This was Tuesday. . . . They would leave by special ship on Thursday morning. . . . They would have several hours in Port Sunlight seeing factories, houses, people, and would be home by Saturday night! His enthusiasm was devastating, and I was sort of sorry to have to point out that he would have to ca' canny: this was the week of the Uig " sacraments." Next week they would be in another parish and would continue in succession round all parishes in the Island. It would be most unwise to attempt to promote a visit to England regardless of the respect accorded to Comanachadh in Lewis, and, anyway, no person of influence in the community would absent himself on such occasions. So his Lordship had to curb his ardour until the circuit of holy ordinances had been duly solemnised. Then he did actually organise a visit to Port Sunlight by a large company of prominent men selected from the various townships: a luxurious holiday which they greatly enjoyed. At Port Sunlight, too, they were impressed by much of what they saw and heard; so much so, indeed, that some of them admitted to me later that they were nearly dazzled into siding with Lord Leverhulme. But as they " contemplated " on the voyage northwards and drew nearer to the little *dachaidh* (home) on the Island, somehow the Port Sunlight impression got blurred. By the time they landed at Stornoway it had vanished completely; and the sentiment of the deputies in the whole matter was succinctly expressed by Ruairidh Chaluim:

" *Ach an deigh na h-uile car, cha' neil càl an sud ach an tràilleachd!* " (" But after all, there is nothing yonder but slavery! ")

It may seem strange that so able a man should be so pathetically incapable of understanding the native mentality and point of view. Hence the absurd assumption by Lord Leverhulme of the title " Lord of the Western Isles." And he would live up to that dignity, too: he would have a piper to play appropriate tunes while he dined. When not engaged in playing the bagpipes the man was expected to work in the gardens; in itself a solecism of which his Lordship was innocent of all knowledge—but an indignity which, it must be admitted, caused no undue concern to this modern MacCrimmon!

On a spring evening, after contributing the measure of music deemed necessary for the creation of proper atmosphere and flow of digestive juices, Donald wished respectfully to have a word with his Lordship.

" Well, what is it, my man? "

" Well, my Lord. I was just wanting to tell you that in a fortnight it will be time to be planting the potatoes, and I will have to be going home then to put them down, but if the weather is right I will finish the job in a week and will be ready to come back then."

" But you are now in regular employment! I pay you a good wage! I provide you with good food. You are not hard worked. You now earn as much money in a week as will buy sufficient potatoes for you and your family for a year. I require you here. *I cannot agree to let you off for a week to plant potatoes.*"

" But, Lord Leverhulme, the potatoes must be planted ! I will need to go home and plant them at the right time ! "

" Listen to what I say, my man. I am giving you good advice. You had better take it. If you do not—if you go without my consent—you should clearly understand that by so doing you will lose your job : I shall have no further need of your services."

It was with no small degree of self-satisfaction his Lordship told me next day the story of how he had made the foolish fellow see sense. For, to the ultimate threat of dismissal, Donald had merely given a " Very good, my Lord," and continued in the dual capacity of piper and gardener. But when his Lordship sat down to dine a fortnight later there was no music to stimulate the juices. Donald was late ! His Lordship was annoyed. He gave instructions that Donald should immediately play the pipes. But back from the kitchen came astounding information : *Donald had left word that he had gone home to plant the potatoes—and would not be coming back !*

.   .   .   .

The full story of the influences and undercurrents of local diplomacy which ultimately succeeded in transferring Lord Leverhulme's affections and creative urge from Lewis to Harris would make interesting telling, but as many of the people concerned are still very much alive I will refrain from mentioning names. Not that there is anything discreditable to anyone in what was done; rather the other way about. But even then I feel sure that the principal actors would prefer to remain in modest obscurity. And in any case my purpose in attempting a brief résumé of an interesting episode in Hebridean history is not so much to show up faults or virtues on either side as to bring into relief the fundamental differences in their respective philosophies and ideologies.

For more than a year it had been obvious to some men in Harris that things were not going well with Lord Leverhulme's schemes on the sister isle: that indeed, because of his lordship's refusal to establish any further crofts in Lewis, his schemes were meeting such strong opposition that he must be feeling sore about the whole business and probably looking for a way of escape that would not involve loss of face. So, over a dram, two or three of the worthies put their heads together and concocted a letter purporting to be written on behalf of the people of Harris. (It is more than doubtful if the latter knew anything about the letter, but that is by the way.)

The people of Harris had watched with great interest his Lordship's efforts on behalf of Lewis; and how deeply they deplored the failure of the people of Lewis to appreciate and grasp their opportunity! If only his Lordship would consider coming to *Harris*—where, they ventured to suggest, the natural scope for development was even greater than in Lewis, what a different reception he would receive from the people there!

The letter couldn't have arrived at a better time. It came as solace to a vexed soul. Had he not often heard it said that the people of Harris were quite different from the people of Lewis! True, so far as his own observations had gone, the two peoples were quite indistinguishable. But here was the proof of the difference! Obviously the people of Harris were kindly, appreciative, shrewd. *They* knew which side of their bread had the butter!

This was a matter for further investigation. He would like to meet these people. He did: a huge gathering of them who came in response to the fiery-cross summons initiated by the " delegates " immediately on receipt of the letter from Lord Leverhulme requesting the favour of a meeting. Just what the purpose of the meeting was, was not at all clear to the great majority before starting out for the rendezvous. But when his Lordship at the outset thanked the people of Harris for their so very kind letter (by the way, this was the first time they had heard of it!) it did not take the astute Hearachs long to grasp that something big might be afoot, and they played up nobly. It was a great meeting—utterly free of the bickerings and disputations so characteristic of meetings with the people of Lewis. Nor was it without its emotional moments, which were as a balm to his Lordship's smarting wounds.

But in business, emotion was a treacherous guide. They must be practical. What were the facts?—distances from fishing grounds, etc.? Ample information on such points was immediately forthcoming.

A safe and suitable harbour?—After all, Stornoway in Lewis was a good harbour!

They agreed: Stornoway was indeed a good centre. Yes—but what about Obbe in Harris? Wasn't it even more central to the fishing grounds than Stornoway? True, Obbe had a disadvantage in the dozens of tidally submerged rocks outside its harbour in the Sound of Harris. Yes, but surely a few rocks like that would not stand for long in the way of a man of Lord Leverhulme's forceful genius!

This was stimulating talk indeed. Nor was his Lordship dismayed by those rocks. Not a bit—they might have been deposited there by the Creator just to give the opportunity one day of showing the greatness of His creature. Pouff! What was dynamite or gelignite for if not for blowing obstacles out of the way of reformers?

Clearly here was a way out of the Lewis impasse. Here was a people who appreciated him; who would appreciate schemes he might set a-going for the betterment of themselves and their island. He would come again with his experts to examine the problems and practicable possibilities on the spot. And so it came to pass. He was like a small boy with plenty of money in his pocket looking at a fascinating toy in a shop window. Soon his mind was made up: he must have that toy. So he bought the whole of South and East Harris, extending to many thousands of acres of which an incredible portion is bare rock and bleak mountain on which even heather cannot grow—although, surprisingly, in between the rocky ledges there is indeed a growth of short, sweet, fine fescue grass beloved by Black-face sheep, which yield the finest-quality mutton in the world.

But it was the harvest of the sea that was the great attraction; and the vision of his great fishing fleets bringing in their silvery cargoes for the plenishing of the breakfast tables of the world was the genesis and inspiration of all his schemes in the Hebrides.

. . . .

Exasperated, frustrated and finally sickened by the stubborn refusal of the people of Lewis to give adequate support to his schemes because of an incomprehensible regard for their wretched little crofts, the opportunity now opened to him in Harris rekindled in Lord Leverhulme the blaze of enthusiasm for adventure and " progress." That the people of Harris might be equally foolishly attached to their even more wretched little crofts was to his Lordship unthinkable; and the people of Harris were much too astute to bring so delicate a subject into the discussion: if a good milk-cow came offering its services to the island their concern should be, not to frighten it away, but to milk it; and to that task they heartily applied themselves.

There followed such a stir of activity as Harris had never known—nor is likely to see again. The harbour had to be enlarged, involving the blasting away of those rocks. A new pier of a size adequate to cope with the future large volume of shipping must be built. A modern town would be established on the bare slopes surrounding the harbour—a town in which the streets must not be straight and in which no two houses must be identical in plan. A cinema, clubroom, offices, shops . . . Roads converging on the new metropolis must be improved, and new roads made. Then there was the cannery that had recently been erected near Stornoway—that would be taken down stone by stone and beam by beam, transported to Obbe and re-erected there.

Some of the local officials who had previously gone about their business at the leisurely, decorous pace characteristic of the Hebrides, suddenly found themselves caught up in an incredible whirl of activity. The local road surveyor—a man who had never before found full scope for his really great ability—as consulting architect for the new proprietor was one of these. Plans and estimates, and still more plans and estimates to satisfy the voracious appetite of the inspired reformer, were constantly being called for. Soon a juvenile staff of assistants had to be recruited and special furniture bought for holding the ever-growing pile of plans and estimates.

One of the troubles of the architect (or *was* it really a trouble?) was that Lord Leverhulme was by way of being an authority on art and architecture himself, and therefore prone to argument and change of mind in such matters. A plan of a building or a street or whatever it was would be agreed on one day. But in the small hours of next morning the alert mind of his Lordship might detect in it a flaw or two. Ah! that must be studied again on the spot. So to the architect would go the urgent message,

" Meet me on ground ten to-day with Plan 5007." And off the architect, with Plan 5007 and note-book, would rush to reach the rendezvous in time.

Hm—yes: it's obvious now that you see it; that window is too high and too near the door—must be altered accordingly.

Certainly: appropriate alterations sketched on plan and noted in book.

Then this bend in the road?—too sharp—widen it—*so*.

Quite, but that will seriously encroach on site of proposed house !

Well, that cannot be helped; must have adequate curve on road—erase house.

House erased from town plan.

And so on for two hectic hours resulting in urgent necessity for several more plans and estimates. A heartbreaking man to work for ! But of course there was the brighter side to such exasperations—and the surveyor carried on with a cheerful heart.

Hundreds in Harris joined the pick-and-shovel brigade, mending and constructing roads, digging foundations; tradesmen, too (pucka and pseudo) were busy building bridges, piers and houses. There was a well-paid and not over-strenuous job for every able-bodied man on the island.

But to the Highlander at home continuous application to manual labour soon becomes monotonous: after all, if the labourer is worthy of his hire is he not also worthy of reasonable leisure for contemplation? Absenteeism was creeping in.

This would never do ! It might jeopardise his schemes ! The danger must be effectively countered. It was—very astutely. To everyone who would give satisfactory service up to a specified standard and for a stated period there would be presented a paid-up life insurance policy of amounts ranging from £100 to £500. That was a real incentive that worked like magic. Would present-day Minister of Labour please note?

Soon, though, the anxiety was on the other side: the man was getting old—more whimsical and unpredictable every day. *What if he suddenly lost interest in the Harris schemes!* Not but some of the schemes might be daft enough; but that wasn't the point. The really important thing was that easily earned weekly pay-packet. Something must be done to safeguard that . . .

The "delegates," under inspiration of another dram or two, concocted another letter. This one said the people of Harris desired to put before him a proposal of a purely personal nature which they ventured to believe might be of interest to his Lordship.

Again the fiery cross went round; again the people of Harris responded in force—and again they were curious to know what it was they wished to see his Lordship about.

The first few words uttered by his Lordship shed a bright light on the mystery, and they loudly cheered! He referred to their desire, as expressed in their wonderfully kind letter: their desire to show to him and to posterity their profound appreciation of what he had done for them and their island. He could scarcely find words to express his appreciation of their appreciation! He was moved—deeply moved—by so wonderful a gesture (actually with a handkerchief he had to wipe away the tears). The suggestion that their purpose might be most appropriately achieved by naming the main centre of his activities (which was Obbe) after him was particularly attractive, and he would of course be delighted to defer to their wish. But—if he might?—he would like to make just one suggestion. He observed that the suggestion in the letter was that the new name should be " Levertown." Now (as somewhat of a connoisseur in such matters) he must be frank with his friends by admitting to them that "Levertown" rather jarred his musical ear; there was a plebeian note in it! But "Leverburgh," now? That to him sounded just right; and if they did not mind . . . ?

No! Not at all! They were grateful for the suggestion! *Of course* "Leverburgh" was the right name! Hear, hear! Loud cheers.

And so it was that the old hamlet of Obbe died and the new town of Leverburgh was born.

The new pier was completed. To it came ships carrying bricks, timber, ironmongery, steel girders, lime, cement and the thousand other things requisite for the creation of the new régime. Leverburgh was fast becoming a town in embryo, and generally the transformation of Harris went on with undiminished speed. But his interests were many and far-spread. A visit to West Africa became an urgent necessity. Full directions for the prosecution of the works in Harris during his absence were duly given. Reluctantly he proceeded to that far-off land of palm nut oil; but he would return to his beloved Harris at the earliest possible moment.

Then one day to Harris there came a telegram with the shocking intimation that Lord Leverhulme had died, and that all activities on the island were to cease forthwith!

Nor were they ever resumed. From the day of his death it was a process of disintegration and shutting down and finishing up of everything that Lord Leverhulme had done and planned for Harris.

It took many months for the people to adapt themselves to the sudden vacuum which succeeded the stir. Nor was the loss of the pay-packet now the only regret. For, towards this strange little man of dynamic personality and unbounded courage and resource there had grown up among the islanders a degree of respect that was almost affection. He might be tyrannical—oh, yes! But he could also be kind, in his own way; and he was terribly clever.

Leverburgh never attained the stature of a town: just a score or so of houses and some scars on the moor (now healed by kindly time and vegetation) where streets and buildings were meant to be.

And the pier—that imposing structure of piles and planks that seemed to cover acres. Three years ago, when I landed there off a motor-boat from Berneray the piles were rotting and the planks sagging to such an extent that we were glad to get off them on to firm land. The last I have heard of it—quite recently—is that about a year ago the Local Authority, to whom its dangerous condition was an embarrassment, sold it to a company of Harris crofters, who have sawn it into boards and battens and fencing stobs and firewood for sale in the neighbourhood; and rumour has it that the crofters made a modicum of profit on the deal.

True Celtic philosophers that they are, in due course the people of Harris settled down to their wonted pace and way of life. So far as they and their island are concerned, by and large, Lord Leverhulme might not have been. And is it not something to be profoundly thankful for that, despite repeated attempts to convert a free and forthright people to the status of city serfs, they are still essentially free to maintain and develop that God-given individuality in human life and outlook which elsewhere is being so ruthlessly smothered?—that in respect of our Highlands and Highland people we can still rejoice that no tyrant sound of factory horn offends their tranquil air?

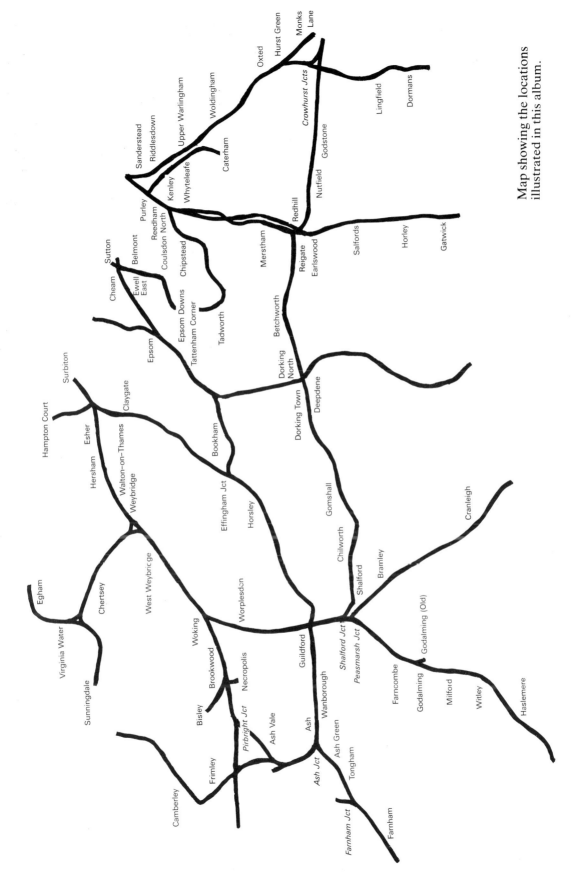

Map showing the locations illustrated in this album.

CONTENTS

INDEX

INTRODUCTION

Celebrating steam in Surrey has produced some surprises. One of them is finding so many pictures of steam trains at work on lines which were electrified many years ago. I suppose part of the reason is that the exceptional train worked by steam was a novelty and worth a picture. Despite this I have failed to turn up any steam pictures at some of the county's stations, so if your local one or your favourite spot isn't here, please forgive me. Another point I must make is that the county's boundaries have changed down the years, so I have had to make up my mind where Surrey begins and ends. So far as the London & South Western and London, Brighton & South Coast railways' main lines are concerned the main changes have been at the London end, and I have chosen to start my coverage at Surbiton and Purley respectively.

Because Surrey adjoins London, two of the earliest trunk lines to the south had to pass through it on their way to Southampton, Brighton and Dover. It also meant that London's growth led to house building and general urban development, with the railway being associated with this activity very closely. In some places the railway came first. Surrey has more suburban than main line stations and lots of examples of the station starting life as the point of communication with the outside world for that particular community, and then losing that status as the road network grew. Happily for railway lovers there are very few closed stations, while only three branches have been lost completely, two of which were semi-private anyway. Is that why there is no preserved railway in the county?

I have grouped the pictures in five sections corresponding fairly closely with the original line ownership, which dictated the train service pattern. The merging of the three main railway companies into the Southern Railway in 1923 didn't bring many changes to where the trains started and finished, neither did the changeover to electric traction which began in the 1920s, though it vastly increased the number of passenger trains. At the beginning of each section there is a brief outline of its railway history, brief because the detailed information is readily available elsewhere, but it may be of interest to have some of the background in outline with the dates of local opening and electrification. There is more information in the captions, about which I must say that I have tried to be accurate but make absolutely no claim to infallibility. Rather the reverse. I'm sure you will find interesting things which I don't mention and you must put that down to my ignorance.

The basic book on Surrey's railways is C.F. Dendy Marshall's *History of the Southern Railway*. It can be supplemented by the three volume history of the LBSCR by J.T. Howard Turner and R.A. Williams' two volumes on the LSWR, which alas only take the story to 1900. Some branches and sections have been described in smaller and more local works, *The Caterham Railway* by J. Spence being an example. There is no extensive book on the third company which made up the Southern Railway in 1923, the South Eastern & Chatham. Of general books which include Surrey railways in their surveys of Southern England those by H.P. White and Edwin Course can be consulted with profit. On signalling, locomotives, and rolling stock we have been well served in recent years, by George Pryer, D.L. Bradley, and P.J. Newbury to name only three. New books of great and detailed learning about every visible aspect of the railway heritage seem to appear almost monthly, so there is no shortage of reference material, though LSWR carriages still await their biographer. Lastly there are the Middleton Press companions to this book: *Branch Lines to East Grinstead*, to *Tunbridge Wells*, and to *Horsham*; and in the *Southern Main Lines* series: *Woking to Portsmouth* and *Epsom to Horsham*. In them, some of the places which receive summary treatment in this book get justice.

A lot of these pictures are credited to fellow photographers, to whom I now express my thanks for putting up with my importunity and for letting their work be used. With a number of stations Ian Leith of the Royal Commission on Historical Monuments saved the day when I despaired of finding anything to show you, thanks to his mastery of the Rokeby Collection. Uncredited pictures are either my own taking or from my collection. Lastly as always we have to thank Neil Stanyon for reading the proofs, and Norman Langridge for delving into his ticket collection to delight us yet again with the unusual.

Peter Hay
Hove 1986

1 THE OXTED LINE: SANDERSTEAD TO DORMANS

The Oxted line is among the youngest pictured in this book. After the building of the Brighton main line in the late 1830s, and the promotion of the South Eastern Railway direct line from London through Sevenoaks to Tonbridge in 1862, both companies began to eye the territory between them, despite a 'non-aggression pact' signed in 1848. There was a false start in the 1860s when the independent Surrey & Sussex Junction Railway (covertly backed by the LBSCR) began work on a route from South Croydon towards Tunbridge Wells, but this was brought to a halt by the financial crisis of 1866/67 and the self-righteous rage of the SER at this attempted poaching. It took ten years for the matter of a line through this area to come alive

again, and this time the LBSCR consulted its rival before the latter could feel that the old adversary was up to its tricks again. As a result things went more smoothly and the line was constructed, partly along the previous route through Oxted, but then veering south to East Grinstead. The SER took up its option of being a partner in the northern half and the Croydon & Oxted Joint line was born in 1884, lasting until 1923 when both its owners became part of the new Southern Railway. The line from Hurst Green junction was solely LBSCR, with a connection to the SER at Crowhurst junction west of Edenbridge.

None of the lines which focused on Oxted were electrified under the great SR schemes of the 1930s and until the diesels came in the

1. With Sanderstead station just visible beyond the bridge, a typical Oxted line formation of the early 1950s sets off for Riddlesdown, its next stop. This is the 4.44 pm East Croydon to Tunbridge Wells West and Tonbridge via Edenbridge Town, with a 'Maunsell Mogul' (N class 2–6–0) in charge of a 'Trio' or 'Birdcage' 3-coach set. In time BR standard stock would replace both. (S.C. Nash)

1960s they remained an outpost of steam in Surrey, bringing regular daily steam workings into the LBSC or 'Central Section' portions of Victoria and London Bridge. There was also the added attraction from time to time of steam 'specials' to Lingfield race meetings.

Trains serving Oxted were not tightly timed, though until the advent of modern 2–6–4 tanks, courtesy of BR, they could provide a stiff task for ageing LBSC engines, often the only power available. Probably the best known of the down trains were those leaving Victoria just before 4 o'clock in the afternoon, and just after 6pm. During the latter years of steam working the heavy '6.10' as it was then known, attracted quite a following because it was sharply timed amid the electrics to East Croydon, and then faced the stiff climb to Oxted tunnel. Most other trains on the Oxted line took their time. My favourite was the 4.20pm London Bridge to Brighton via East Grinstead. I could photograph it on New Cross bank, take a local electric up to London Bridge and catch the 'City

Limited' down to the coast. Then, as the 4.20 arrived at Brighton an hour after me, there was time to go somewhere out on the Lewes line and take another picture of the same train, well worth the effort if one of the famous 'Brighton Atlantics' was working it.

In the end steam gave way to diesel working. All this was despite at least two solemn assurances, before and after World War II, that the Oxted - East Grinstead - Haywards Heath route was to be electrified. BR is at last, it would appear, carrying out part of these promises, half a century after they were first made. All the stations in Surrey remain open, though Monks Lane Halt was an early casualty of the war. From serving mainly to bring country gentry (and milk) up to Town, the lines through Oxted have developed a commuter business. This time it looks as if the electrics really will get to East Grinstead. Further information and pictures of the section south of Oxted can be found in *Branch Lines to East Grinstead* and *Branch Lines to Tunbridge Wells*.

2. By the end of the 1950s many of the workings through Oxted were powered by BR class 4MT 2–6–4 tanks built at Brighton. When no. 80148 arrived at Riddlesdown with a train for Victoria in 1960, there were still few BR carriages on these services. This one has a post-war Bulleid coach in the lead, followed by a pre-war Southern Railway 4-coach corridor set. (J.H.W. Kent)

3. The Q class 0–6–0s were designed by R.E.L. Maunsell for the SR in 1937 and a pair in original condition can be seen in picture 70. In the late 1940s Maunsell's successor, O.V.S. Bulleid, fitted them with wide diameter chimneys and in that form several came to the Oxted line . No. 30549 was subjected to yet another alteration which produced the hideous chimney seen here at Upper Warlingham, where it was shunting coal wagons in 1960. (J.H.W. Kent)

London Brighton & South Coast Railway.

Marden Park to

Dormans

Three-engine train

HERE is another example of the tardiness of British Railways' Southern Region services (this page, November 4).

On one journey, the 6.10 from Victoria to Uckfield, Sussex, became a relay train.

It arrived 25 minutes behind time at Edenbridge. There a second engine was added: this caused another nine minutes delay. At Eridge, the second engine was replaced by a third.

The train reached Uckfield 58 minutes late.

1907 engine

What was the cause? Say British Railways: "Bad coal has a lot to do with it."

And the engines?

The first engine was built in 1911, the second in 1908 (there are 45 of this class still in commission), and the third in 1907—rebuilt in 1919.

Comments an official defensively: "Some engines older than these are still in use."

1947 troubles on the Oxted line: the engines were 2421, a Brighton Atlantic; an I3 class 4–4–2 tank; and a C2X class Vulcan goods 0–6–0.

4. The signalman's view of a Victoria to Eridge and Brighton train passing his box at Woldingham. In 1960 the three disc headcode denoted that this service would reach Eridge by way of Edenbridge Town. The engine is BR standard 4–6–0 no. 75070 with a mixture of SR and BR carriages.
(J.H.W. Kent)

5. Another look at the south end of Woldingham, the last intermediate station on the Croydon & Oxted Joint line, taken from the top of the wall seen in picture 4. By March 1967 diesel trains had taken over the regular workings, but the Locomotive Club of Great Britain secured no. 34102 *Lapford* for parts of its "Surrey Downsman" railtour. It was one of the last 'West Country' class engines still working in its original form. Until 1894 Woldingham was called Marden Park.
(J. Scrace)

6. The postcard from which this view of Oxted station was obtained is postmarked 1907, so we can take this to represent the Edwardian scene. Milk of course was still travelling in churns, empty back to the country on this platform and full ones going to Town from the opposite side. The wheelbarrow looks too horticultural to be part of Oxted's official equipment.

7. As BR standard 4–6–0 no. 75075 leaves with a train from London Bridge, we can just glimpse the engine of the 'Oxted Motor' standing in the bay platform behind the signal box. In 1960 the box had seen some years since its last painting, and the stain down the weatherboarding below the nearest window shows where the signalman habitually emptied the dregs of their tea. (J.H.W. Kent)

8. Hurst Green has grown in importance since this picture was taken in 1957. Some of the changes are shown in *Branch Lines to East Grinstead* and among the sadder losses are the two LBSCR junction home signals which frame class 4 tank no. 42088 as it heads south on the East Grinstead line. (J.H.W. Kent)

9. 'All that was left of it'. Monks Lane Halt was opened in 1907 and closed in 1939, though for a while this ghostly reminder endured. The construction was typical of the LBSCR 'motor halts', and when any of them was removed it left very little trace of its passing.

←

10. Edenbridge tunnel is unusual in that it has *four* mouths. In fact it is technically two tunnels with a railway bridge built between them to carry a line crossing at right angles. This is the Redhill - Tonbridge line from which this picture looking north through the 'north' tunnel is taken. Just disappearing from view is the Tunbridge Wells West to Oxted pull and push train. (J.H.W. Kent)

11. At the south 'south end' of Edenbridge tunnel we can see that the crew of this engine have forgotten to put up any white route indicating discs to announce where they are taking their smart red and cream train. I expect the signalmen knew anyway. (J.H.W. Kent)

12. 'Back favourites for a place' was the standard advice the porter at Lingfield used to give punters who asked him for tips about the horses. In 1961 N class 2–6–0 no. 31854 has brought the racegoers down from Victoria and they stream hopefully across the foot-bridge (now on the Bluebell Line) towards their afternoon's sport. (D.W. Winkworth)

London Brighton & South Coast Railway

Oxted to

Norwood Junc.

13. Collars and ties, sports jackets and flannels; the attire of the gentlemen waiting on this platform while an up train runs in, firmly places this picture of Dormans station in the 1930s. The fact that the engine, one of the famous LBSCR class L 'Baltic' tanks, has not yet been rebuilt to a tender engine takes us back before 1936. The platforms are backed by substantially braced wooden screens and provided with bench seating for a multitude, making Dormans a little unusual among LBSCR stations.
(R.C.H.M./Rokeby collection)

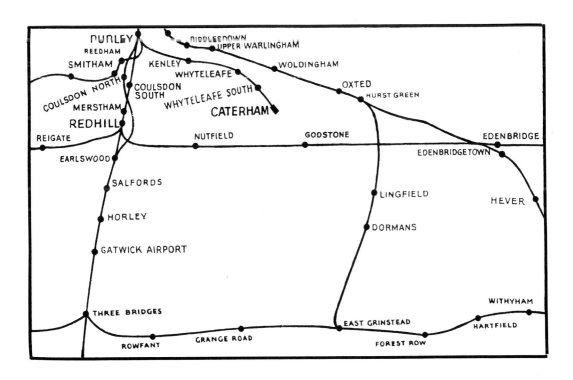

2 THE BRIGHTON MAIN LINE AND BRANCHES

The Surrey portion of the main line to Brighton is physically simple but complex in terms of Victorian 'railway politics'. Parliament in the mid-1830s was asked to sanction both a line to Brighton, and one to Dover by the SER, each using the London & Greenwich and the London & Croydon railways at the northern end. To avoid what was then considered wasteful duplication the divergence of the Brighton and Dover routes was eventually fixed south of the North Downs at Redhill. In the complicated legal dance which followed the SER bought the Redhill to Coulsdon section from the Brighton company, which retained the Coulsdon-Norwood portion. Coulsdon (South), Merstham and Redhill were SER stations as a result. With

the opening of the line to Guildford in 1849 Redhill became a junction of importance, and very soon a byword for delay, sometimes unavoidable but often, during periods of tension between the two companies, suspected of being not without malice. The South Eastern controlled Redhill, and the Brighton trains suffered. By the 1890s the line south from Croydon was choking with trains and the LBSCR's patience was exhausted. It therefore quadrupled the route from Croydon to the mouth of the Chipstead valley where it built its own station, the delightfully named Stoat's Nest, some distance short of the SER Coulsdon station. From Stoat's Nest (recently closed as Coulsdon North) the 'Brighton' struck out with an independent

14. A Brighton express romps past the old Purley North signal box early this century. The disc with the cross bars over the buffer indicates it is routed via the new Quarry line, and every lamp iron not otherwise occupied has been used to store engine headlamps.

Leading the train is a 'Pullman Pup', a six-wheeled luggage van-cum-electricity generator providing lighting for the Pullmans behind. The engine is B4 class 4–4–0 no.60 built in 1901 and patriotically named *Kimberley*.

route through the North Downs to Earlswood, by-passing the SER and all its works. It became known as the Quarry line by virtue of passing near the Merstham chalk quarries, ultimate destination of Surrey's (and the world's) first public railway, the Surrey Iron Railway of 1802. By 1907 four tracks were in use on from Earlswood to the Sussex boundary, and electrification took place in 1933.

The Brighton main line has two Surrey branches, both built by the SER. The first appeared in 1856, south eastwards up the Caterham valley from Purley (called Caterham Junction until 1888) which was electrified in 1928. Secondly, leaving Purley by a burrowing junction under the main line, the Tattenham Corner branch commenced operations as far as Kingswood in 1897. Opening to Tadworth followed in 1900, and they finally reached Tattenham Corner in 1901. I believe the chairman of the by then South Eastern and Chatham Railways Managing Committee, Sir Henry Cosmo Bonsor, had a lot of land in the area, but whatever the reason for making the line it certainly opened up some lovely country for a day out. But it

took time, because after 1914 the line beyond Tadworth was only used for race trains until the spread of London suburbia made it worth electrifying the whole branch in 1928.

Although the SR operated what were, in all but name, electric locomotives between 1925 and 1929 on the Coulsdon and Wallington electric services, all goods and parcels trains were steam worked. The first proper third rail electric locomotive appeared in 1941 and there were still only three of them by 1949, so even on the Brighton main line, steam trains were quite common until the 1960s. Apart from the Newhaven Boat trains there was the daily Hastings-Birkenhead service between Brighton and Redhill, and the early morning paper train from London Bridge also carried passengers. The old SER influence persisted by virtue of the steam-hauled 5.25 pm London Bridge to Reading and Tonbridge which divided at Redhill after running down non-stop to Coulsdon South, the SER station of 1889. Only Reading line passengers enjoyed a corresponding through service up in the morning. At weekends in the summer quite a number of steam-worked

15. The duty number SPL1 on the buffer-beam disc shows that this M7 class 0–4–4 tank from Nine Elms was not passing Kenley in the everyday course of its duties. In fact, it is on its way to Caterham to work a rail tour in July 1964. The quality of station architecture on this branch is due to its promotion by a local group, independent of the South Eastern Railway. (S.C. Nash)

regular and excursion trains from the Western, Eastern, and London Midland Regions also traversed the Brighton line. A high point in the year was Derby Week, when the Royal train brought steam to Tattenham Corner for the Derby and the Oaks. The return to the Palace was by road, but even the empty Pullmans going back to London attracted attention. The Caterham branch was denied these marvels and had to be content with a daily steam-hauled coal train.

16. In the early 1960s the only steam trains regularly seen on the branch to Caterham were those serving coal depots along the line. Just before Christmas 1963, Q1 class 0–6–0 no. 33018 brings the modern equivalent of Yule logs to the valley under its dusting of snow. A modern nameplate on the end of the signal box has replaced the earlier one which was placed in a frame on the front, behind the railings. (E. Wilmshurst)

18. In 1956 the Caterham branch celebrated its centenary with a special train, SECR carriages hauled by an LBSCR engine. That's not a ghost on the footplate, it's the Locomotive Inspector in fancy dress and false whiskers. Pulling the train is the Locomotive Works shunter from Brighton, which enjoyed Stroudley livery for years. Somebody over-ordered when its predecessor was so painted on being restored for preservation in 1947; what better use for the surplus? (S.C. Nash)

17. One of the results of the South Eastern and LCDR joint management was profits, here seen invested in some respectable carriages for the Charing Cross train which is waiting to leave Caterham about 1910. The engine is one of Stirling's F class, downgraded from more important work by newer engines which the shareholders could now afford. (Lens of Sutton)

19. As housing spread down the valley from Croydon it seemed worthwhile to cater for it by opening Reedham Halt in 1911. The trains went only as far as Tadworth until electrification and when this train from Charing Cross called in May 1926, one week after the end of the General Strike, the halt's surroundings were still quite sylvan. The wooden platforms and oil lamps were replaced after electrification. (H.C. Casserley)

20. The SECR pattern nameboard can be seen on the front of Chipstead signal box as the branch train stands at the up platform. Outside peak hours it was generally necessary to change at Purley for London. The engine is H class 0–4–4 tank no. A162 with an interesting train in tow. The two end carriages are 6-wheeled four compartment brakes, with four short bogie coaches between them; they look suspiciously like SER stock of the 1890s. Chipstead looks very spruce and permanent, compared with bucolic Reedham Halt. The early turn (shift) signalman in the summer of 1926 came to work on his bicycle before the arrival of the first train at 5.48 am. (H.C. Casserley)

21. Tadworth was the branch terminus (except for racing traffic) until the electrics came in 1928, the initial push to Tattenham Corner having produced very little business. The date of this picture is uncerain but the engine is an SER type 0–4–4 tank so it could be in the hopeful years when the extension had a timetabled steam service, 1901 to 1914. The facilities provided were not skimped, though passengers arriving from Town in the dark had many more lamp posts to light their way along the platform than those joining an up train here.
(Lens of Sutton)

22. Tattenham Corner station came to life – and indeed opulence, judging by the Pullmans – with the Derby meeting at Epsom. The ample siding accommodation is all needed and although there may seem to be too many staff about, they will all be occupied once the last race has been run, the

winnings collected, and crowds throng the station. This is either 1922 or 1923 because we can just see the tenders of N class 2-6-0s nos. 812 and 817 (the latter built in 1922), neither of them yet given Southern Railway numbers. (Lens of Sutton)

23. Her Majesty has departed for the course and everybody can relax a little. All has gone without a hitch, so now Schools class no. 30908 *Westminster* can be uncoupled from the four gleaming Pullmans, to turn on the turntable and take them back empty to Stewarts Lane depot at Battersea. It is 4th June 1958.

➤

24. Coulsdon North station was closed in October 1983, having been the terminating point for outer suburban services since the main line was quadrupled south of Croydon in 1899. It was called Stoats Nest until 1911, with this engine shed to provide shelter for a small number of tank locomotives. When overhead electric traction arrived in 1925, its importance declined and this picture is thought to date from then. On view is an LBSC class I1 4–4–2 tank, no. B4. Somewhat unkindly the shed appears to support one end of the gantry carrying the wire for the usurping electrics. (Brighton Library)

➤

25. The Quarry line avoiding the Redhill blockage was opened with the new century, carving through the North Downs alongside but above the old line, which can just be seen on the left. The new crossed over the old on a skew bridge and the tail of this northbound goods is just leaving the curve by which it was approached. In 1922 the load consists of: a 'roader' brake van (with side loading doors it could be used to carry small consignments on quiet branch lines); three open wagons with bulky loads sheeted; some general goods; and then the inevitable string of coal trucks going back empty to the collieries. This collection would not have taxed the nearly new K class 2–6–0, no. 347.

26. A notable southbound train on the Quarry line appears about half a mile south of the one seen in the previous picture. The 'Sunny South Special' began a through service from Liverpool, Manchester and the Midlands to Brighton and Eastbourne in 1904 and became a great institution on the line. It was the first of the 'avoid London' services which the railways seem to reinvent every generation. As B4 class no. 61 climbs the last mile to the summit in Quarry tunnel, the passengers in the third vehicle, an LNWR 'Luncheon and Tea Car' will just be passing the sandwiches.

27. In the background of this 1967 view, steam is pouring out of the mouth of Merstham tunnel (on the original line) after the passage of the preserved LNER 2–6–0, no. 3442 *The Great Marquess*. We are just north of Merstham Station and the white gate beside the train once led to Peters' siding, serving the lime works and quarry which gave the new line its name. (John Scrace)

28. The roses in bloom cannot conceal the fact that this is Merstham station on the old or 'Redhill' line and it is appropriate that the train is a South Eastern section service. The engine is an SER class F 4–4–0 rebuilt with a normal cab and a domed boiler into class F1 in 1907, but the leading van appears to have a London, Chatham & Dover Railway profile. In July 1926 the probability is that this train came from Reading or Tonbridge. (H.C. Casserley)

29. It may be fitted with motor car lighting, but it *is* a steam engine. To be more precise *Dom* started life as the engine part of a Sentinel steam railcar, on the Jersey Eastern Railway in the Channel Islands. Then it worked at Peters Siding (see picture 27) and finally at the Standard Brick Company, whose sidings left the Redhill line at Holme-thorpe signal box between Redhill and Merstham and crossed to and under the Quarry line.

30. With steam lines approaching it from east and west, Redhill was something of a Mecca for enthusiasts until the diesels came. Many of the trains reversing there were worked by engines built before the 1923 grouping of railways, and sought by photographers in their last years at work. Of the four locomotives visible in this picture, three come into that prized category. There will be trouble soon for the driver of no. 31247 as he leaves with the 10.40 am Ashford to Reading in August 1957, for he has a newly painted engine *head*lamp on the buffer beam and some zealous colleague will accuse him of not removing his *tail* lamp when he backed onto his train.

31. Another Reading train stands at Redhill's gaslit platform 1, headed this time by an ex-LSWR engine, T9 class 4–4–0 no. 30310. In 1952 it was a rare treat to ride in the leading 'birdcage' lookout, from where the activities on the footplate were fully visible over the low tender.

→

32. This special train from Brighton to the Midlands via Clapham Jct. and Kensington is on the first part of the Quarry line, just entering Redhill tunnel. On the left is Redhill goods yard and on the right an N class 2–6–0 is approaching Redhill station on the original main line with a van train. The Schools class making good time with a twelve coach load is no. 30909 *St. Paul's*, still rated for express work in 1958.

→

33. Earlswood's platforms on the Fast lines saw few passengers, as most of the trains calling at the station ran via Redhill and used the Slow line platforms on the right. The up express is hauled by no. 38, the second member of D.E. Marsh's original series of Atlantics. Until he built the 'balloon' or elliptical roof stock from 1905 onwards, LBSCR carriages tended to be rather dwarfed by any Pullman cars in the train. By the pristine look of the surroundings this picture may date from 1906, when Earlswood got a new station. (Brighton Library)

35. When the main line was quadrupled south of Earlswood, Horley was considered sufficiently important to warrant a new station, opened in 1906 about ¼ mile south of the one which this train is leaving. It would appear that the road crossing is to be replaced by a bridge reached by a new embankment (already completed) which is set back from the existing track to allow the new down Fast line to be built. The engine is another B4 class 4–4–0, working an Eastbourne train. (Lens of Sutton)

34. The halt at Salfords was opened in 1915 with Slow line platforms only, connected by this footbridge with a factory on the down side whose workers were its only customers. The service remained confined to them until electrification in July 1932 when it appeared as Salfords Halt in the public timetable for the first time. It never gained platforms on the Fast line which Battle of Britain class no. 34083 *605 Squadron* is using, with a train for the London Midland Region via the West London line. (J.H.W. Kent)

36. There have been several pictures of the B4 class in this section, and when one of them was broken up in 1950 on the up sidings south of Horley, no. 2074 took its revenge by over-powering the crane which had picked up its dismembered front section. The crane was in fact older than the engine, having been made for the LCDR by Cowans, Sheldon & Co. in 1899, and it lived to lift another day, until 1962. (Brighton Library)

37. Carrying the sporting classes to the races had been a moneyspinner for the Brighton railway from the beginning, so when Croydon steeplechase was replaced in 1891 by a new course south of Horley, the railway opened a station nearby at Gatwick, the racecourse owner contributing £5000. Enlarged when the line was quadrupled, it normally served only race trains, though there was an unadvertised stop there in the morning for golfers, by the Horsham-Horley 'motors'. After a period of disuse, the place has blossomed into a very busy station indeed with the building of Gatwick Airport. There are no golfers now. (Lens of Sutton)

Wednesday and Thursday, March 6th & 7th.

GATWICK STEEPLECHASES.

51   GATWICK BOOKINGS.—Passengers for Gatwick will present at the Booking Office a voucher showing the date and Train by which they are authorised to travel and Booking Clerks and others concerned must issue tickets in exchange for these vouchers at the present ordinary fares only on the date and by the Train named thereon.   Similar vouchers will be presented at Gatwick Station for admission to the platforms for the return journey.   These vouchers may be accepted at intermediate Stations where the Train by which they are available calls, and tickets issued in exchange accordingly.   Ordinary Tickets, card or paper, may be issued in exchange for the special vouchers.

Officers of His Majesty's Forces, in uniform, may be booked to Gatwick without vouchers, and if A.F.W. **3504** is surrendered, a Government Rate Ticket may be issued at the reduced rate (1916 basis); if no concession voucher is surrendered, a Government Rate paper ticket must be issued but the full 1917 public fare charged.   Ordinary tickets must not in any circumstances be issued to Officers in uniform.

Passengers without Vouchers, or presenting Vouchers for use by a Train otherwise than indicated thereon must not be booked.

The foregoing instructions do not apply to Racecourse Staff and Police or to Messrs. Bertram & Co.'s Catering Staff, who will travel by the Trains shown in Sections 52, 53 and 55.

[COPY OF VOUCHER.]

GATWICK STEEPLECHASES. First Day, March 6th, 1918.	Issued to—	Subscription Series of Race Meetings, Under National Hunt Rules.				Voucher to be retained by the HOLDER and used to admit to the Platform for the (§) p.m. Train from Gatwick to	Voucher to be retained by Booking Clerk.
		GATWICK MARCH STEEPLECHASES, 1918, First Day, Wednesday, March 6th.					GATWICK STEEPLECHASES, First Day, March 6th, 1918.
				s.	d.	VICTORIA.	
		Reserved Enclosure	– – –	20	0	—	Please issue to bearer a Return Ticket to Gatwick by the (§) a.m. Train from London Bridge, L.B. & S.C. Ry., on payment of the present day Ordinary Fare, at the time of Booking.
		Entertainment Tax	– – –	2	6	GATWICK	
			Total	22	6	STEEPLECHASES,	
		PRATT & COY., Clerks of the Course.				First Day,	
		This Ticket is issued subject to the National Hunt Rules.				March 6th, 1918.	

§ Here will appear the Time of the Train by which the holder is entitled to travel.

52   LONDON BRIDGE TO GATWICK AND BACK.—On both days of this Meeting Messrs. Bertram and Co.'s Staff (about 80 Third Class) will travel from London Bridge to Gatwick by the 7.25 a.m. and 8.7 a.m. Trains, Passengers by the latter changing at East Croydon into the 8.25 a.m. from Victoria.   Returning from Gatwick by the Train leaving Brighton at 3.53 p.m.

On Thursday a Van will be sent from Gatwick to London Bridge by the 3.53 p.m. Train from Brighton.

53   VICTORIA TO GATWICK AND BACK.—Gatwick Race Course Staff, about 110 Third Class, will travel from Victoria to Gatwick by the 8.25 a.m. Train and return to London Bridge by the 3.53 p.m. Train from Brighton.

1918 Arrangements for Gatwick Spring Steeplechases: such pleasures continued at home although the Second Battle of the Somme was only three weeks away.

3 SOUTH FROM SUTTON

Sutton station is at the junction of four lines, the importance of which has varied down the years with the pattern of train services. The first station was opened in 1847 when an extension of the London & Croydon Railway from their (West) Croydon station to Epsom was built. The L&CR had become part of the newly created LBSCR in 1846. Ten years later the LSWR had also reached Epsom by a line from Wimbledon, and in slightly wary union with the LBSCR was pushing south to Leatherhead, reached in 1859. It was rather like two cats jointly stalking a mouse and wondering which was going to have the eating of it, because Leatherhead was not the real prize. The capturing in 1859 of the Direct Portsmouth Railway by the LSWR had altered the balance of advantage at Portsmouth in its favour, and the LBSCR in consequence wished to shorten its own route to Portsmouth, which was then a round-about one via Brighton. It hoped to do this by building south from Leatherhead to Dorking, on to Horsham, and south to its West Coast line. By 1863 it had succeeded. Sutton was thus on the new LBSCR Mid Sussex route, and was no longer served only by local trains.

In addition to these developments to the south, there had also been changes to the north of the town. In the early 1860s before the 1866 banking crisis brought a minor 'railway mania' to an abrupt end the London Chatham & Dover Railway, emboldened by its success in reaching London while the SER's back was turned, was looking for fresh worlds to conquer, and its roving eye lit on the as yet undeveloped stretch of South London and Surrey between Herne Hill and Epsom Downs. Given the 'Chatham's' financial condition, then and subsequently, the LBSCR really ought not to have been

38. The Epsom Downs branch received Pullman specials in Derby week. They started from Victoria and had to negotiate a nasty 1 in 90 climb into Sutton station, especially trying if the train was stopped on the bank at the junction home signal. In the sunlit 1930s an LBSCR class E5 0–6–2 tank and an SECR class H 0–4–4 tank share the burden of lifting 'Race Special 145' across the junction and into Sutton. The leading engine is no. 2573. (Lens of Sutton)

alarmed though I suppose there was always the possibility of some other railway company invading the area if the LCDR did not. It went on all the time in those days, so in 1862 the LBSCR obtained powers to build south westwards from the Peckham area through Mitcham to Sutton, with the soon absorbed Banstead & Epsom Downs Railway continuing up towards the racecourse. By the end of the 1860s the Peckham-Epsom Downs route was open and connected to the several other lines which it crossed on its way. The final development of railways in the area south from Sutton was the opening in 1885 of the LSWR line from Leatherhead to Effingham Junction, which is really part of the story of the New Guildford line.

Although the Sutton-Horsham-Mid Sussex line did partly re-establish LBSCR influence in Portsmouth, so far as the Sutton area was concerned, the Epsom Downs branch was quite a jewel in the company's crown. In Victorian times Epsom Downs was a popular place for a summer day's outing by South Londoners, while the Derby race meeting attracted not only gigantic crowds, but Royalty. Queen Victoria was no race-goer, but the Prince of Wales as leader of fashionable society often came. Royal use of the SECR Tattenham Corner line was a more recent innovation, so there are many pictures of the LBSCR Royal train 'going to the races'. There were also Pullman specials for 'the nobs', and so many more humble extra trains that the branch had three signal boxes which only opened for race traffic. Prosaically they were called A, B, and C Intermediate. What a pity Belmont station's first name of California was not perpetuated for one of them.

All the lines south from Sutton were electrified before the war, the 1925 Leatherhead to Dorking electrics using the former LSWR route from Epsom to Waterloo. Overhead wire AC electric traction of the LBSCR type reached Sutton from the Croydon direction

39. One of the early LBSCR Rail Motors at Belmont, supposedly on its first day of operation, 11th June 1906, with a brand new 'Balloon' trailer car which cost £750. From its leading end the driver controlled Terrier no. 661 by air-operated remote control gear.

The LV (last vehicle) board is a daylight substitute for a tail lamp and standing beside it is the Conductor Guard with his satchel for issuing tickets if necessary.
(Brighton Library)

the same year, but was changed to the standard SR kind in 1929 when the line from Peckham Rye via Mitcham Junction was electrified. Nevertheless, steam engines continued to use the route, even after it was electrified all the way through Horsham to the Sussex coast in 1938. This ended, at least for passenger trains, many years of toiling up to the summit by milepost 28 on the Forest Ridge between Holmwood and Ockley, and many years of making up lost time going down the other side. (It is said that in her funeral train the Old Queen travelled faster in death than she ever had in life, coming down the bank from Holmwood into Dork-

ing that rainy morning in 1901.) Goods and parcels services continued to be steam worked, but the most interesting and notorious steam train carried the morning papers with a few benighted passengers. It left London Bridge some time after 5 am and finally reached Brighton (via Dorking and Horsham) in time for a late breakfast. *Not the best way to get from London to Brighton* unless you were sleeping off a night on the town. I don't think the all-Pullman steam specials to Epsom Downs survived World War II and indeed in 1982 the branch was reduced to single track after fire destroyed Epsom Downs signal box.

40. Although the engine is working hard to get this Pullman race special up the 1 in 58 through Belmont station, there is no trace of smoke from no. 2091, last of the famous I3 class 4–4–2 tanks. The signalman is enjoying the spectacle of this elegant train.
(Brighton Library)

41. This faded picture of Epsom Downs station dates from 1873/4 and shows the state of things either during a race meeting or on a Bank Holiday. All the engines have been turned to face London, and only the one in the very centre is by Stroudley, one of his 1872-built 2–4–0s. Everything else is by his predecessor at Brighton, J.C. Craven who had 'done well for himself' and retired in 1870.

42. Derby Day 1907 at Epsom Downs. The LBSCR Royal Train on the left has brought King Edward VII to the races behind the new I1 class 4–4–2 tank no. 600, but not all the other engines have used the turntable. Most are E5 class 0–6–2 tanks with high arched cab roofs, seen from the signal box which con-trolled this unusual layout. Among the novelties we should note the engine holding sidings between the lines serving platforms 3 and 4, and 5 and 6, terminating in earth bank buffer stops. They were removed after elec-trification rendered them redundant.

43. A closer look at one of the superb LBSCR bracket signals at Epsom Downs. Placing a stop signal (for arriving trains) at the outer end of the platform would cause chaos if it was obeyed as such. I suspect its true purpose was to indicate if the line was clear all the way to the buffer stops, and not to bring the incoming train to a stand. An engine siding once occupied the space between the tracks in the foreground.

44. A rail tour in June 1966 brought crowds to Epsom Downs once again, behind Battle of Britain class no. 34089 *602 Squadron*. It has a 6 coach train but the electrics were often 8 cars, passengers for Banstead and Belmont being instructed to use the front 4. (J. Scrace)

45. The Epsom end of Sutton station provides a somewhat enclosed setting for an excursion from the Midlands to the Sussex coast, about 1960. The engine with W 708 obscuring its numberplate is an LMS type class 5 4–6–0 and the carriages are also LMS pattern. (Lens of Sutton)

46. In 1911 four tracks replaced the previous double line from just west of Sutton to the country end of Cheam station which was rebuilt with platforms only on the outer tracks. Platforms for the inner tracks never materialised, hence the appearance of this lengthy boarded foot crossing from one side to the other. One of Stroudley's Gladstone class 0–4–2s heads a down train about 1911. (Lens of Sutton)

47. A Victoria to Portsmouth train sweeps through Cheam on the Fast Line, which has no electric 'third' rails. By the unused condition of the live rail of the platform line this picture must date from 1928/29, the electric service through Cheam beginning in March 1929. The engine is B4 class no. B65 with some nice 'Brighton' carriages and signals also visible. (Brighton Library)

48. The 'Porcupine train' in this picture is one with a vehicle that has a projecting fan of flexible spikes. It is being run through Ewell East while checking clearances between trains and lineside structures on the Sutton to Dorking line. As this is not a high speed activity the work is entrusted to an LBSCR goods engine, C2X class no. 32546. (Lens of Sutton)

49. The LBSCR station at Epsom (Epsom Town after 1923) also boasted a small engine shed for suburban tank engines, like the one in the down siding. As an up Portsmouth to London Bridge train goes by, hauled by Gladstone class no. B174 and entirely composed of 'balloon' stock, the fireman of the tank engine is trimming the coal in its bunker. This picture is dated 18th March 1928, a year before all traffic was concentrated at the new Epsom station built on the site of the former LSWR one. (H.C. Casserley)

LONDON AND SOUTH WESTERN RAILWAY.

TELEPHONE NO.
520 EPSOM.

(486 D)

EPSOM STATION,

....191.........

DEAR SIR,

....RACES,.......................

      I beg to inform you that Race Horses can leave this station at...................... m. on..,

due...at...............m.,

via..

      Please advise me of any horse-boxes you may require as early as possible, and oblige,

                           Yours faithfully,

50. Epsom station's new signal box towered above the platforms, seen in the distance as yet another C2X approaches with a goods working from Leatherhead. The siding in the left foreground once served an engine turntable, long gone by July 1960. (D. Clayton)

51. Signalling between Epsom and Ashtead was assisted by the provision in 1899 of Epsom Common signal box. It stood by the down line, and in June 1955 a 'Vulcan' goods with the double dome boiler called briefly, to set down some stores. Signalmen who came to work on bicycles used the gate in the fence for access. (D. Clayton)

52. Despite the electric rails steam working by push-and-pull trains like this continued to provide the service south from Dorking until 1938, when the 1925 electrification was extended to the coast. A Stroudley D1 class 0–4–2 tank is pushing a Billinton 6-wheeled luggage brake and a pair of 'Balloons'. As the B prefix to the engine's number has been replaced by the figure 2 this view must date from after 1931. (Lens of Sutton)

53. Excursions from outside the Southern Region continued to bring steam to the Dorking line well into BR days, for example when Battle of Britain class no. 34077 *41 Squadron* took over a train from West Drayton to Bognor Regis on 14th June 1958. As the driver attacks the climb to Betchworth tunnel on his way to the summit south of Holmwood, he has steam to spare and a 350-ton load is no worry. (J. Scrace)

54. This picture was also taken from just south of Dorking station, the camera being positioned by the wooden fence of the footpath and gaining a low level view of a Stroudley E1 class 0–6–0 goods tank setting off up the bank to Holmwood. The date is about 1911. (Brighton Library)

55. With steam shut off and a 'white feather' showing at the safety valves, B4 class no. 57 runs down past the hay siding at Dorking with a Portsmouth to London Bridge train. The carriages are all Edwardian vintage gas-lit stock, the uniformity of the train's appearance providing a most pleasing ensemble. (Lens of Sutton)

4 THE 'SOUTH WESTERN' IN SURREY

The London & Southampton Railway was opened from Nine Elms, London, to Woking on 21st May 1838. Actually they had intended to open on 1st June but as the Derby meeting occurred in the preceding week they decided to turn an honest penny by advancing the opening of their line, advertising no less than eight race trains. These were to run to what was officially Kingston station (unofficially Kingston-upon-Railway) and since 1877, Surbiton, which was then the only station anywhere near Epsom. The Special Traffic Department, which ever afterwards was an important part of the operating executive, got its baptism of fire on Derby Day. Over 5000 people turned up at Nine Elms and the station, the staff, and the trains were overwhelmed with excited race-goers. How many actually got to the races and how they were got home again, history does not record, but the L&SR had started something which was ever afterwards a money spinner. Undeterred by the deluge of humanity that day at Nine Elms, or perhaps realising they were, in racing parlance, 'on to a good thing', within a few weeks they were offering 'Woking for Ascot Races' and LSWR, SR, and BR have been doing well out of the race traffic ever since.

The line was opened onwards from Woking Common to Winchfield in Hampshire early in the autumn of 1838. Traffic far exceeded expectations and the growth was maintained well into the 1850s by opening branches from the main line. The first was from Woking to Guildford in 1845, followed in 1848 by another from Weybridge to Chertsey, and in 1849 from Surbiton to the south bank of the Thames opposite Hampton Court. Thereafter right into the 1860s most years saw the LSWR (as the London & Southampton had become in 1839) opening a new line in north west Surrey or across the river in Middlesex. These extensions greatly increased the company's capital debt but secured its territory against serious invasion.

56. Surbiton station was rebuilt by the SR late in the 1930s, very much in the style of the time, the clock tower and the lift tower being specially noticeable. They still looked modern in 1953 when Lord Nelson class no. 30865 *Sir John Hawkins* raced up the through line bound for Waterloo with an express from Bournemouth. There is a Bulleid three-set leading and the whole train looks very smart in its red and cream livery. (J.H.W. Kent)

The story of the LSWR in Surrey includes the 1885 New Guildford line from Hampton Court junction west of Surbiton, through Effingham Junction, where a connection with Leatherhead was made, to Guildford. As the towns served grew and became dormitories for London it prospered, being fully electrified in 1925. Similar glory never shone upon two other branches from the main line, both commencing at Brookwood. One ran north through Surrey heathland to Bisley Camp. The 1¼ mile National Rifle Association Bisley Common Tramway was first used in 1890, and by Royalty in the elegant shape of the Prince and Princess of Wales. Thereafter the LSWR and its successors worked the 'Bisley Bullet' as the branch train was affectionately known, until the line closed in 1952. Brookwood's other branch was very different in character. The London Necropolis & National Mausoleum Company was formed in 1854 to provide a commercial burying ground in rural Surrey, London's churchyards being completely full. At first there was no station on the main line and the

daily train from Waterloo ran to Necropolis junction where it reversed into the cemetery. There were two stations: a North one was for Non-conformist and Roman Catholic funerals while Anglicans used the South station several hundred yards further on. The train served both. There was also a private station adjoining Waterloo, bombed during the war. The funeral train has not run since 1941. Alas both Brookwood's unusual branches have long been lifted.

Thanks to its rapid expansion in the mid-Victorian years the LSWR was never seriously challenged in north west Surrey during the nineteenth century. When the Metropolitan District Railway shook off its steam-induced lethargy and electrified its services early in the new century however, the South Western scented danger. What if the now-electric District chose to extend its line south westwards? The LSWR, already losing traffic to the new electric trams, began its own programme of electrification. Although delayed by World War I, the conversion of the Portsmouth Direct and New

57. A King Arthur on a down West of England train in full cry at Surbiton. No. 30745 *Tintagel* was one of the first series of this class, the 'Urie Arthurs' built for the LSWR, and in 1950 was in Southern Railway green, only the new numbers on the cab and

the numberplate recognising nationalisation. The first carriage, a pre-war Maunsell third which has been used to augment a popular train, is still in SR green too. There is no platform on the down through line at Surbiton. (J.H.W. Kent)

Guildford lines, as well as those services north of the main line, was completed by 1939. Extension of the third rail over the county boundary into Hampshire on the main line itself had to wait till 1967, giving another generation of Surrey boys (and their fathers) the exciting specacle of a steam-hauled express in full cry, passing their suburban platforms.

Victorian railways had to keep a watchful eye constantly open for predators in the shape of other companies out to poach part of their business. The skirmishes with the LBSCR in the Epsom-Leatherhead area are one example, and the unexpected arrival on the scene of the South Eastern Railway as purchasers of the Reading, Guildford & Reigate Railway in 1852 showed what could

happen if your attention wandered. LSWR apprehension about the final ownership of the Portsmouth Railway (Godalming to Havant) is understandable, especially when there was talk of a connecting link with the SER near Guildford. Already competing with the LBSCR for the favours of Portsmouth, the South Western feared it would have to contend with South Eastern competition as well. Bracing itself for rage and reprisals from the 'Brighton' it leased the Portsmouth line in 1858 and, after scuffles at Havant, began a Waterloo to Portsmouth service. It took the best part of a century, I fancy, before any of its owners made much money out of the Portsmouth Direct line. Southern Main Lines: *Woking to Portsmouth* (Middleton Press) looks at it in detail.

58. Rebuilt West Country pacific no. 34022 *Exmoor* represents the final generation of steam power on the LSWR main line, as it passes Esher with the 10.30am Waterloo to Bournemouth express in 1963. The fine layout of the main line with the fast tracks in the centre positively encouraged fast running, even though on the down line there is a steady rise all the way out to the county boundary near Brookwood.

60. A famous Surrey spectacle before the war was the all-Pullman Bournemouth Belle, seen here passing Hersham with a Saturday load of twelve cars, probably well over the 400-ton weight limit for the Southern Railway's most powerful engines, the Lord Nelson class. No. 852 *Sir Walter Raleigh* in green and the Pullmans in the umber and cream must have been a sight to see in 1939. (C.R.L. Coles)

59. The first generation of six-coupled express engines were designed for the LSWR by Dugald Drummond and were not a success. Only one class, the T14, was retained after the King Arthurs were built, and they were tinkered with for years before they could be called reliable. They worked various humdrum duties – no. 447 is shunting at Esher with the local goods – but were scrapped after the war. (C.R.L. Coles)

61. There is considerable similarity between SR Bulleid carriages and the early BR standard stock, as we can see in this picture of a Bournemouth line train in 1965. Having been reduced to the slow line for part of its journey, rebuilt Merchant Navy class 4–6–2 no. 35030 *Elder-Dempster Lines* is crossing back to the fast line here at Walton-on-Thames. (Lens of Sutton)

63. The kink in the tracks approaching Weybridge was formed when two tracks were increased to four early this century, but it does not seem to have slowed BR Standard class 4 no. 75075 on this short Basingstoke train. In May 1958 there are both steam and electric carriages of Bulleid's design on view. (E. Gamblin)

62. Weybridge station in the 'silk hat' era, before the four tracks extended this far out from Waterloo. The bay platform on the right was once much used by trains from the Chertsey line terminating here. The track is ballasted above the sleepers, which made the running quieter but concealed rotten wood. (Lens of Sutton)

64. On Saturdays in the summer mixed traffic engines like H15 class no. 524 were pressed into express service. This boat train to Southampton includes a Pullman car and carries reporting number 231 to help signalmen like the one here at Byfleet junction know which train it is. The line on the right joining the down slow comes from Chertsey, and West Weybridge station (now Byfleet and New Haw) is in the smoke beyond the signal box. (C.R.L. Coles)

65. Woking station was rebuilt in 1937/8, in concrete like Surbiton, and complete with lift towers. The West Country Pacific in the Bulleid green livery is 21C105 *Barnstaple*, built in July 1945 and given a conventional number (34005) in May 1948, so this picture probably dates from the last summer of the Southern Railway, 1947. (Lens of Sutton)

66. The west end of the layout at Woking from 'Tin Bridges' shows the up yard full of goods wagons, by comparison with picture 5 in *Southern Main Lines: Woking to Portsmouth*. There are also four tracks and an electricity substation. Using a T14 class 4–6–0 on a Basingstoke slow with Bulleid carriages indicates the late 1940s as the date. (Lens of Sutton)

67. Appropriately, it was under a steady drizzle that the Necropolis train was photographed amid the gloomy laurels of Brookwood cemetery. This is the North station and the train is approaching from the (Anglican) South station, so we can deduce that the last rites have been observed and all concerned are making their way back to London. The Victorian description of all this, scenery and behaviour, would have been 'tasteful'. (R.C.H.M./Rokeby Collection)

68. The last run of the 'Bisley Bullet' was a special organised on 23rd November 1952. With photographers in attendance the two LSWR carriages built for the Plymouth-Turnchapel line are propelled out of Brookwood station towards Bisley by M7 class no. 30027. Entrances barred by folding metal gates make fine places to stand on the journey.

London and South Western Ry.

787

TO

Brookwood

69. The special train alongside the grass-grown platform at Bisley, once again with photographers scattering the late autumn leaves. The tail lamp *was* removed before the run back to Brookwood. There was once a three mile extension of the tramway beyond the white gates in the distance, but in 1952 it had been closed for nearly 30 years.

70. Double heading by two of the SR class Q 0–6–0s was not something commonly seen on the LSWR main line, where the S15 class 4–6–0s handled all the really heavy work, but the date of August 1941 for this picture suggests a reason for using two engines. Other results of the war are cab side windows plated over, and the blackout anti-glare curtains which can be seen beside the drivers. The location is Pirbright. (Lens of Sutton)

71. The awnings over Egham's platforms are something of an LSWR standard pattern, the one on the up side being longer to shelter the larger number of passengers who would be waiting for a train to Waterloo, like the one arriving behind an M7 tank. (R.C.H.M./Rokeby collection)

72. Was the photographer who recorded this Ascot Race Special near Virginia Water the railwayman whose onions are doing so well on his lineside allotment? It is Coronation Year, 1911, when Royal Ascot was an especially glittering occasion. Next to that it seems prosaic to record that the train is worked by a 'Large Hopper', the nickname for Drummond's L11 class 4–4–0s. (Lens of Sutton)

73. The imposing engine which dominates this view of Chertsey station is the tank engine version of Urie's H15 class 4–6–0s, the H16 class 4–6–2 tanks which were built in 1921/2 to work the increasingly heavy transfer goods trains between the new Feltham marshalling yard and those on the northern lines. Although at one time they worked race trains to Ascot, by 1954 their passenger work was mainly confined to rail tours.

74. Surrey pinewoods formed the background for this Reading-Waterloo train as it arrived at Sunningdale one sunny day in 1934. The engine is another L11 4–4–0, with an LBSC carriage leading LSWR stock, and its headcode indicates a route via Staines and Twickenham, rather than Weybridge and the main line. (C.R.L. Coles)

75. Camberley was served by trains from Waterloo to Woking via Ascot and Pirbright Jct., and by an Ascot-Aldershot-Farnham service. The latter appears on this old picture postcard, the engine being an Adams outside cylinder 4–4–2 tank of the '0415' class, still to be seen on the Bluebell Railway. (R.C.H.M./Rokeby collection)

76. A later picture, taken this century, shows the Ascot-Farnham train again, this time running into Frimley station behind an 0-4-4 tank. The white patch on the left bridge abutment makes it easier to pick out the position of the signal at the end of the platform. (R.C.H.M./Rokeby collection)

77. Ash Vale station during the war, with a soldier in uniform, white rings on the awning supports to make them more visible in the blackout, and a Bulleid 'austerity' or Q1 class 0-6-0 built in 1942 to aid the wartime traffic on the SR. Even in peace time Ash Vale station sees lots of soldiers because of its proximity to Aldershot.
(R.C.H.M./Rokeby collection)

78. Farnham's first electric trains appeared
in 1937, the same year as Egham and two
years before the Camberley line, so this view
of a two coach push-and-pull train arriving
must date from the early 1930s. Once again
the engine is an 0–4–4 tank (M7 class) on
which the LSWR depended in steam days for
suburban and branch line work.
(R.C.H.M./Rokeby collection)

79. Retracing our steps towards London we see an up parcels train passing a down electric at Farnham Jct. The Aldershot line runs to the left of the still camouflaged substation and the single line branch to Tongham

(Goods) diverges to the right. Until the line
from Pirbright Jct. through Aldershot was
opened in 1870, Guildford-Farnham trains
ran via Tongham. (Lens of Sutton)

80. Although Tongham was from 1855 the station for Aldershot, it declined in importance after 1870 and lost its passenger trains in 1937. In 1956 goods trains still called and the up platform retained its awning, just in case there should be a change of heart. All was lost from 2nd January 1961 when final closure took place. The engine is U class 2–6–0 no. 31630. (E. Wilmshurst)

81. REC on the headcode disc stands for Railway Enthusiasts Club, organisers of 'The Compass Rose' railtour of West Surrey on 5th October 1957. LSWR class M 7 tank no. 30051 worked an LBSC pull-and-push set, here standing at Ash Green Halt on the Tongham branch. (R.N. Thornton)

82. The Tongham branch goods leaving the Guildford line at Ash Junction where the SER Reading line diverged behind the diminutive LSWR signal box. Having had to accommodate SER trains from Ash Junction to Guildford since 1849, the LSWR got its own back after 1870 for its trains used the SER line from Aldershot Junction South to Ash Junction, on their way from Farnham to Guildford. (Lens of Sutton)

→

84. A rail tour train at Wanborough in 1957, about to leave for Ash Junction and the Tongham goods line. (R.N. Thornton)

83. Wanborough was included in the electrification scheme which commenced on New Year's Day 1939, but continued to see regular steam trains until January 1965 when the Reading to Redhill service was taken over by the 'Tadpole' diesel units. In November of 1966 BR Standard class 5 no. 73065 passed through on a special train from London Victoria to Westbury in Wiltshire, via Redhill and Reading. (J. Scrace)

85. It is to be hoped that the Adams Jubilee (0–4–2 class A12) which is entering Worplesdon station with a down train will not be working all the way to Portsmouth tender first. It is more likely either that this is a short working from Woking or that the engine has been commandeered to replace a failure and will be coming off at Guildford. Comparison with picture 12 in *Southern Main Lines: Woking to Portsmouth* will show that Worplesdon station hasn't changed much down the years, though the schoolboys will look rather different by now.
(R.C.H.M./Rokeby collection)

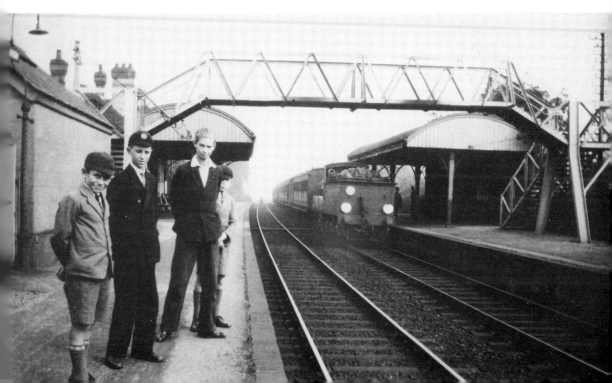

NEW GUILDFORD, SURBITON, LEATHERHEAD, EPSOM AND WATERLOO LINE.

London and South Western and London Brighton and South Coast Companies' Trains.

WEEK DAYS (continued). STATIONS.	65 Pass. T		66 Pass. L		67 Goods. C L		68 Goods. B		68a Engine. Sats. excepted.		69		70 Pass.		71 Pass. L		72 Pass. B		73		74 Pass. B	
	arr.	dep.	arr.	dep.	arr.	dep.	arr.	dep.	arr.	dep.	arr.	dep.	arr.	dep.	arr.	dep.	arr.	dep.	arr.	dep.	arr.	dep.
	p.m.	p.m.	p.m.	p.m.	p.m.	p.m.	p.m.	p.m.	p.m.	p.m.	p.m.	p.m.	p.m.	p.m.	p.m.	p.m.	p.m.	p.m.	p.m.	p.m.	p.m.	p.m.
Guildford	...	4 33	...	4 52	...	...	...	...	...	...	...	...	...	...	...	6 3	...	...	...	...	...	...
London Road, Guildford	4 37	4 38	4 56	4 57	...	...	...	...	...	...	...	...	...	...	...	...	...	...	...	...	...	...
Merrow Sidings	...	...	...	...	...	...	...	...	...	...	...	...	...	...	...	...	...	...	...	...	...	...
Clandon	4 45	4 46	5 4	5 5	...	...	...	...	...	...	...	...	...	6 35	...	...	...	...	...	...	...	...
Horsley	4 53	4 55	5 12	5 14	...	...	...	...	...	...	...	...	6 37	6 38	...	...	...	...	...	...	...	...
Effingham Junction	4 58	4 59	5 17	5 18	...	...	...	...	...	...	...	...	...	...	...	...	...	...	...	...	...	...
Bookham	...	...	5 22	5 23	...	...	...	...	...	6 15	...	...	...	...	6 20	6 21	...	...	...	...	...	...
Leatherhead (L.B. & S.C.)	...	...	...	...	...	...	...	5 49	...	...	...	...	...	...	...	...	...	8 26	...	...	...	6 54
Leatherh'd (S.W.)	...	...	5 28	5 33	...	5 10	...	...	6 20	...	...	...	...	...	6 26	6 30	...	...	...	...	...	...
Ashtead	...	...	5 37	5 38	...	5 15	...	...	...	...	...	...	...	...	6 34	6 35	6 30	6 31	...	...	...	...
Epsom	...	...	5 43	5 45	5 21	5 50	6 2	...	...	...	...	...	...	...	6 40	6 42	6 35	...	...	...	7 0	...
Ewell	...	...	5 48	5 49	5 54	6 55	...	...	...	...	...	...	...	...	6 45	6 46	...	...	...	...	...	...
Cunliffe's Sidings	...	...	...	...	7 1	7 10	...	...	...	...	...	...	...	...	...	...	...	...	...	...	...	...
Worcester Park	...	...	5 54	5 55	7 15	7 20	...	...	...	...	...	...	...	...	6 51	6 52	...	...	...	...	...	...
Cobham & Stoke d'Abn.	5 3	5 4	...	...	...	...	...	...	...	...	...	...	6 42	6 43	...	...	...	...	...	...	...	...
Oxshott and Fair Mile	5 9	5 10	...	...	...	...	...	...	...	...	...	...	6 47	6 48	...	...	...	...	...	...	...	...
Claygate and Claremont	5 14	5 15	...	...	...	...	...	...	...	...	...	...	6 53	6 54	...	...	...	...	...	...	...	...
Hampton Court Junction	5 18	...	...	...	...	...	...	...	...	...	...	...	6 57	...	...	...	...	...	...	...	...	...
Surbiton	5 21	5 22	...	...	...	...	...	...	...	...	...	...	7 0	...	...	...	...	...	...	...	...	...
Malden	...	...	...	...	...	...	...	...	...	...	...	...	...	...	...	...	...	...	...	...	...	...
Raynes Park	...	...	5 58	5 59	...	7 25	...	...	...	...	...	...	...	...	...	...	...	...	...	...	...	...
Wimbledon	...	...	6 2	6 4	7 28	...	...	...	...	...	...	...	...	...	6 59	7 1	...	...	...	...	...	...
Earlsfield	...	...	...	6 8	...	...	...	...	...	...	...	...	...	...	...	...	...	...	...	...	...	...
Clapham Junction	5 35	...	6 12	6 18	...	...	...	...	...	...	...	...	...	...	...	...	7 8	7 9	...	...	...	...
Queen's Road	5 37	...	...	6 16	...	...	...	...	...	...	...	...	...	...	...	...	...	...	...	...	...	...
Nine Elms Yard	...	...	...	...	...	...	...	...	...	...	...	...	...	...	...	...	...	...	...	...	...	...
Vauxhall	5 39	5 41	6 18	6 20	...	...	...	...	...	...	...	...	...	...	...	...	7 14	7 17	...	...	...	...
Waterloo	5 46	...	6 25	...	...	...	...	...	...	...	...	...	...	...	...	...	7 22	...	...	...	...	...

WEEK DAYS (continued). STATIONS.	75 Empty Train.		76 Pass. L		77 Pass. B		78		80 Empty.		81 Pass. B		81a Empty. Sats. excepted. A L		82 Goods. B		83 Pass. T		84 Pass. L		85 Goods. B	
	arr.	dep.	arr.	dep.	arr.	dep.	arr.	dep.	arr.	dep.	arr.	dep.	arr.	dep.	arr.	dep.	arr.	dep.	arr.	dep.	arr.	dep.
	p.m.	p.m.	p.m.	p.m.	p.m.	p.m.	p.m.	p.m.	p.m.	p.m.	p.m.	p.m.	p.m.	p.m.	p.m.	p.m.	p.m.	p.m.	p.m.	p.m.	p.m.	p.m.
Guildford	...	...	...	6 47	...	...	...	...	...	...	...	...	...	...	...	...	...	7 20	...	...	...	...
London Road, Guildford	...	...	6 51	6 52	...	...	...	...	...	...	...	...	...	...	...	...	7 24	7 25	...	...	...	...
Merrow Sidings	...	...	...	...	...	...	...	...	...	...	...	...	...	...	...	...	...	...	...	...	...	...
Clandon	...	...	6 58	6 59	...	...	...	...	...	...	...	...	...	...	...	...	7 31	7 32	...	...	...	...
Horsley	...	...	7 6	7 7	...	...	...	...	...	...	...	...	...	...	...	...	7 38	7 39	...	...	...	...
Effingham Junction	...	...	7 10	7 11	...	...	...	...	...	...	...	...	...	...	...	...	7 42	7 43	...	...	...	...
Bookham	...	7 0	7 15	7 16	...	...	...	...	...	...	...	7 35	...	7 45	...	...	...	...	...	...	...	...
Leatherhead (L.B. & S.C.)	...	...	...	...	...	7 30	...	...	...	...	...	7 40	...	...	...	7 45	...	...	...	...	...	8 15
Leatherh'd (S.W.)	7 5	7 7	7 21	7 24	...	...	...	...	7 40	...	...	...	...	7 50	...	...	...	...	...	8 5	...	...
Ashtead	...	7 13	7 28	7 29	7 34	7 35	...	...	...	...	7 44	7 45	...	7 55	7 50	8 0	...	...	8 9	8 10	...	...
Epsom	...	7 19	7 34	7 36	7 39	...	...	...	...	...	...	7 50	8 0	8 A10	8 7	...	...	...	8 15	8 16	...	8 25
Ewell	...	7 23	7 39	7 40	...	...	...	...	...	...	...	...	...	8 14	...	...	...	...	8 19	8 20	...	...
Worcester Park	...	7 28	7 45	7 46	...	...	...	...	...	...	...	...	...	8 19	...	...	...	...	8 25	8 26	...	...
Cobham & Stoke d'Abn.	...	...	...	...	...	...	...	...	...	...	...	...	...	...	...	...	7 47	7 48	...	...	...	...
Oxshott and Fair Mile	...	...	...	...	...	...	...	...	...	...	...	...	...	...	...	...	7 52	7 54	...	...	...	...
Claygate and Claremont	...	...	...	...	...	...	...	...	...	...	...	...	...	...	...	...	7 58	7 59	...	...	...	...
Hampton Court Junction	...	...	...	...	...	...	...	...	...	...	...	...	...	...	...	...	8 2	...	...	...	...	...
Surbiton	...	...	...	...	...	...	...	...	...	...	...	...	...	...	...	...	8 5	8 6	...	...	...	...
Malden	...	...	...	...	...	...	...	...	...	...	...	...	...	...	...	...	...	...	...	...	...	...
Raynes Park	...	7 32	7 49	7 50	...	...	...	...	...	...	...	...	8 23	...	...	...	...	...	8 29	8 30	...	...
Wimbledon	7 35	...	7 53	7 55	...	...	...	...	...	...	...	...	8 26	...	...	...	...	...	8 33	8 35	...	...
Earlsfield	To		7 59	8 0	...	...	...	...	...	...	...	...	8 30	...	...	...	...	...	8 39	8 40	...	...
Clapham Junction	Merton		8 4	8 5	...	...	...	...	...	...	...	...	8 36	...	...	...	8 20	8 21	8 43	8 44	...	...
Queen's Road	Road		8 8	...	...	...	...	...	...	...	...	...	8 38	...	...	...	8 24	...	8 47	...	...	...
Nine Elms Yard	Siding.		...	...	...	...	...	...	...	...	...	...	8 40	...	...	...	...	...	...	...	...	...
Vauxhall	...	...	8 10	8 12	...	...	...	...	...	...	...	...	...	...	...	...	8 28	8 28	8 49	8 51	...	...
Waterloo	...	...	8 17	...	...	...	...	...	...	...	8 A50	...	...	...	...	...	8 33	...	8 56	...	...	...

A Empty Train Bookham to Epsom Light Engine thence to Waterloo

B All Trains marked B are London Brighton and South Coast Company's Trains.

C This Train only runs when required as between Leatherhead and Epsom.

For particulars as to Speed of Trains through Hampton Court Junction, Epsom Junction and Station, see page 2.

86. In 1962 it must have been 70 years or so since the 2–4–0 well tanks of Joseph Beattie last visited the Hampton Court branch, though they were until the late Victorian years the main LSWR suburban engines. Long rusticated to North Cornwall, two of the surviving trio came up to London to work a rail tour in December 1962. I dare say they found Hampton Court station greatly changed. (E. Wilmshurst)

87. After the pre-war electrifications steam trains were few on the New Guildford line. This is the 12.48pm Surbiton to Guildford coal train passing Claygate on 6th April 1965. The engine is another Q1, no. 33018 which selective use of chalk has given back its original number, C18. Claygate's awnings and footbridge are of the familiar LSWR pattern. (J. Scrace)

88. The live rails have arrived in this picture of Bookham, but the electric trains won't be using them till tomorrow. It is 11th July 1925, the last day of steam working and the engine is no. 106, an M7 as usual. The platforms have been lengthened in concrete but the footbridge is that provided for the first passengers in 1885. (Lens of Sutton)

89. The trees, shrubs and grassy platforms combine to make Effingham Junction look as if it is in the Scottish highlands, instead of only 21 miles from Waterloo. The usual M7 tank is working a Guildford via Leatherhead train. (Lens of Sutton)

London and South Western Ry.

757

From _Bookham_

TO

GODALMING (NEW)

90. The New Guildford line of 1885 passed through what was (and I'm sure still is) a part of Surrey which house agents would describe as 'select', the sort of place where Sir Blundell Maple would think it worthwhile to advertise to passengers as they descended the foot-bridge. The train standing at the platform is however the 7.30am Surbiton to Guildford goods, which was allowed 21 minutes for work at Horsley. Perhaps there was some new furniture amongst its load.

91. This goods train is on the up side of the line at Guildford, and is worked by an LBSCR class C3 engine. Many of them were based at Horsham, including B306 which is carrying the Guildford to Horsham headcode, so maybe it is shunting out of the yard before heading south. It still carries the old 'bullseye' type of LBSCR headlamps.

92. At Peasmarsh Junction the Portsmouth line throws off a spur to Horsham, opened in 1865 and closed in 1965. This train is the 1.34 pm from Guildford on 11th May 1963, worked by an LMS-type 2–6–2 tank no. 41303. The trees at the far edge of the meadow on the right are on the never-used embankment from the Redhill-Guildford line to the Portsmouth line. (E. Wilmshurst)

93. A Portsmouth train restarting from Farncombe about 1926. The scene is still strongly LSWR, well after the Grouping, with an M7 tank (no. E47) hauling noncorridor South Western stock. Farncombe West signal box is in the background. (F. Ashdown)

94. The original station at Godalming became Godalming (Old) in 1859 when the Direct Portsmouth line was opened, closed to passengers in 1897 and finally died in the 1970s. It was the terminus of the 1849 line from Guildford. While the passengers on this 1957 railtour inspect the premises, the fireman is up in the bunker of no. 30051 with his hammer, breaking up the larger lumps of coal. (R.N. Thornton)

95. Pictorial evidence suggests that the charming custom of painting alternate boards in the awning valance in contrasting colours was not confined to the Guildford-Portsmouth line in LSWR days. It certainly shows up well in this old postcard of Godalming (New) station, perhaps because the up side awning had just been painted. (Lens of Sutton)

SOUTHERN RAILWAY

FRIDAY, 21st MAY, 1937

Time Table of Special Train

conveying

THEIR MAJESTIES
KING GEORGE VI
AND
QUEEN ELIZABETH
AND SUITE

TIME TABLE

Miles							P.M.
—	PORTSMOUTH DOCKYARD (SOUTH RAILWAY JETTY)	...			}	dep.	2 50
20	PETERSFIELD	...	...	...	...	pass	3 24
44	GUILDFORD	...	...	...	...	pass	3 55
57	LEATHERHEAD	...	...	...	...	pass	4 16
65	SUTTON ...	...	...	...	...	pass	4 30
77	VICTORIA	...	...	...	...	arr.	4 50

96. A down train stopped at Witley on 7th August 1926. The leading engine is one of Adams' celebrated Jubilee (A12) class 0–4–2s, the LSWR mixed traffic engine for decades. Unusually the train engine just peeping into the picture *also* carries the full headcode, which may indicate that the M7 (no. E42) is in trouble and E540 has come to the rescue. The building on the right is the storage shed for Coopers Stick factory. (F. Ashdown)

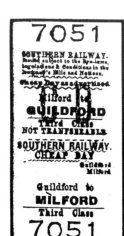

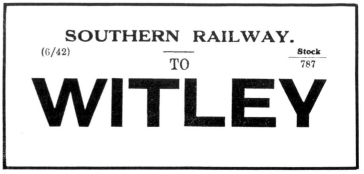

97. A down special passing Haslemere in LSWR days behind an Adams 4–4–0, no. 454. This member of the '445' class was given a new boiler and cab front with round spectacle glasses in 1909 and also a Drummond chimney, which helps to date this picture. Both wagons and wagon sheets on the left are boldly lettered LSWR.
(Lens of Sutton)

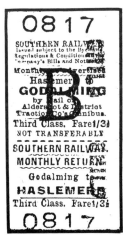

0817
SOUTHERN RAILWAY
Issued subject to the Bye-laws
Regulations & Conditions in the
Company's Bills and Notices
Monthly . . . . . . wherever
Haslemer to
GODALMING
by rail or
Aldershot & District
Traction Co's Omnibus.
Third Class. Fare 1/3½
NOT TRANSFERABLE
SOUTHERN RAILWAY.
MONTHLY RETURN
Godalming to
HASLEMERE
Third Class. Fare 1/3½
0817

SOUTHERN RAILWAY.

(4/39)

Stock
787

TO

HASLEMERE

5 THE 'SOUTH EASTERN' IN SURREY

A 'base line' railway route across Surrey came into being in 1849 when the briefly independent Reading, Guildford & Reigate Railway was opened. As the 'Reigate' in its title referred to the present Redhill station, through west-east communication was established by connecting with the SER 'Old Main Line' route onwards east to Tonbridge in Kent. Reversal at Redhill has always been necessary, at a cost in delays that earned the place the nickname of 'Stopall Junction'. The LBSCR's exasperated reaction has been noted in Chapter 2. West of Guildford, Reading was reached by running powers over the LSWR to Ash Junction and that company gave no opposition when the Reading and Reigate line was taken over by the SER in 1852, though as recorded in the previous chapter it would not have looked kindly at any further extensions of South Eastern influence. It was unruffled so long as the SER refrained from ambitions towards Portsmouth or any other part of the LSWR back garden. This matter happily gave no cause for concern during the Victorian years because the SER was preoccupied with keeping the upstart London Chatham & Dover Railway in its place, and had neither money or inclination to contemplate adventures in Surrey or Hampshire. One shrewd move was linking up with the lordly GWR at Reading, and in time a most useful route to the Channel ports from the Midlands, Wales, and even Merseyside was developed. Generations of railwaymen knew the daily through service as the 'Conti', short for Continental. It was a train that deserved an official title far more than some rather ordinary services elsewhere, which received names in the cause of publicity. Although electric trains have long operated into Guildford, and southwards and westwards from there as well as between

98. The Reading-Tonbridge route has been an east/west artery ever since the Reading connection with the GWR opened in 1858, though the need to reverse at Redhill has always been a nuisance hindering the working there. As part of the railway politics of south east Surrey a double line curve from the LBSCR Oxted-East Grinstead line to the SER Redhill-Tonbridge line at Crowhurst, east of Godstone and not to be confused with a place of the same name on the Hastings line, was built in 1884. Q1 class no. 33003 is just crossing the junction with a Redhill to Tonbridge goods in 1959. (J.H.W. Kent)

Redhill and Reigate, the Shalford Junction to Reigate section and that east of Redhill remained steam territory until the diesels came.

West of Redhill the line has never been easy to work because it was cheaply built and steeply graded over ridges projecting from the foot of the North Downs, most notably around Gomshall. That station is in a dip between two summits, each at the end of a four-mile climb. As the largest passenger engines rarely if ever ran over this line, Gomshall was a welcome sight for many a crew, nursing or flogging their overloaded engine up from Dorking or Shalford. At holiday weekends loads well over 300 tons could be coupled behind a Maunsell Mogul and I'm afraid time was often lost. Probably the hardest turn was the 'Woking Stone', a 500-ton through train of granite ballast from Meldon Quarry on Dartmoor to Tonbridge and points east: see picture 10 in my *Steaming Through Kent*. Wisely it was composed of modern bogie hopper wagons vacuum braked throughout, because the result of *that* lot breaking loose

and running away could have changed the geography of the Guildford district.

There was stone of another kind connected with this line. At Brockham, west of Betchworth, there was once a hearthstone mine, a brickworks, and a chalkpit limeworks, all between the railway and the scarp of the North Downs. Much more notable, and surviving into the 1960s, was the rail system at Betchworth Quarry operated by the Dorking Greystone Lime Co.

Finally this chapter contains pictures of what might well qualify as the county's quietest railway, the Surrey portion of the Horsham and Guildford line. Single track from Christ's Hospital in Sussex to Peasmarsh junction on the Portsmouth line, the LBSCR opened it in 1865 and BR closed it in 1965. What is I think the only abandoned railway tunnel in Surrey took the line into Sussex, between Baynards and Rudgwick. Twenty years later it's still there. *Branch lines to Horsham* describes the whole route in detail.

99. D1 class 4–4–0 no. 31497, homeward bound to Tonbridge with a train from Redhill, restarts from Godstone. This line like its continuation east of Tonbridge is virtually straight, which has tempted many a driver to 'have a go' if his engine was in good trim. The rather straight-sided carriages date from 1929. (J.H.W. Kent)

100. In the background of this view of the Redhill end of Godstone station is the low ridge pierced by Bletchingly tunnel. Comparison of the carriages behind U1 class 2–6–0 no. 31901 with those in the previous picture shows a distinct softening of Maunsell's coach outline, these being 9′0″ stock of 1932. Both photographs were taken in May 1959. (J.H.W. Kent)

101. We can see right through the unusual panelled signal box at Nutfield and on a warm day in 1959 one of the casement type windows is wide open. Few boxes had them; the SER standardising on sash windows and most other companies on horizontally sliding ones. Once again the carriages are the 8′6″ Restriction 1 stock, originally built for main line trains on the former SECR section. (J.H.W. Kent)

102. Completing this look at the accommodation given to passengers on the Redhill-Tonbridge line there is a glimpse of the past in the shape of the 9.06 am leaving Redhill in September 1957. It is a complete SECR train, L class 4–4–0 hauling a 3-coach Birdcage set. Steam rises in the right background from a train leaving on the Reading line and to the right of it is the roof of Redhill engine shed. Sleepers in the foreground are coated, not with early snow, but with sand dropped from wagons from Holmethorpe sidings.

103. As the 1950s drew to a close, withdrawal of branch line services and the coming of new engines caused many old favourites to be placed in store at the back of an engine shed, with sacking tied over their chimneys to keep the rain out. This sad fate has overtaken two E4 class 0–6–2 tanks, nos. 32507 and 32560 which stand marooned at the south end of Redhill shed. Neither has its original pattern boiler, and both are different.

105. A 'three company' train slowing to a stop at Reigate in August 1953. The engine is an LSWR T9 class 4–4–0 which is hauling an SECR Birdcage set, with an SR van bringing up the rear. Electric trains reached Reigate in 1932 but progressed no further.

104. At Redhill in April 1958, a K class 2–6–0 comes through the station on the platformless centre tracks with a Three Bridges to Norwood Junction train of coal empties, a duty that was as old as the railway. It is passing two engines running light to the shed after working in from Reading and Tonbridge. They are M7 class no. 30130 and a Maunsell 2–6–0, both also engaged in a typical Redhill operation. 'B' signal box in the distance was the Redhill nerve centre, controlling access to the Reading and Tonbridge lines which go off to right and left respectively. Semaphore signalling completes the traditional scene.

106. The station building at Betchworth looks to be the work of William Tress, famous for his neo-classical stations on the Hastings line which resembled Gomshall (picture 111), but here he has worked delightfully in the vernacular, a generation before Norman Shaw popularised it. The steeply pitched roofs have red tiles which also adorn the gable end and the upper storey, though the erections to the right are signs of a sad loss of touch by Tress' successors. By May 1964 AWS had been fitted to many SR engines, including no. 31801 which has a shield behind the front coupling and a battery box on the footplating. (J.H.W. Kent)

107. The last relic of the SER Reading-London service was the 7.27 am Reading to London Bridge, here consisting of a Maunsell 3-coach set in red and cream, and two SECR 'swingers' in dark red. N class no. 31864 is working the train in August 1953, ten years before the through service to London finally ceased. On the right we can compare old and new platform heights and above the engine the chimney of the Dorking Greystone Lime Co. indicates more steam, stationary this time, in the enigmatic shape of 'The Perkins' in its shed amid the brambles.

108. A steep standard gauge siding connected the Dorking Greystone Limeworks with the Redhill-Guildford line. Leading from it northwards into the face of the North Downs the lines were on the unusual gauge of 3′2¼″ and along these in 1953 worked a veteran lcomotive, no. 4 *William Finlay*, built in 1880 by Fletcher Jennings & Co. of Whitehaven. After being laid aside in 1955 it eventually found a home at the Amberley Chalk Pits Museum in West Sussex.

109. The modest wooden station at Deepdene was originally called Boxhill & Leatherhead Road, the 'Road' suffix being an indication in the early days of railways that the place named was accessible by direct road from that station. The road was generally a long one. It was renamed Deepdene honouring Thomas Hope's celebrated mansion nearby in 1923, to avoid confusion with the station on the Dorking-Epsom line. In May 1964, this eastbound train was headed by a Maunsell Mogul no. 31866. (J.H.W. Kent)

110. The 7.17 am Maidstone West to Reading coasting to a stop at Dorking (Town) station in July 1956 is formed of an old SECR 'Coppertop' or D class 4–4–0 no. 31549 and a post-1915 SECR Trio set, without 'birdcages'. Do platelayers still carry small amounts of ballast in wicker baskets like the one in the foreground?

111. The SER liking for stations with staggered platforms appeared on the Redhill-Guildford line, and passengers have to cross the line at Gomshall by a boarded crossing from one ramp to the other. As this station is in a dip between two summits, non-stopping trains can be going quite fast and the warning notice is a vital necessity. By August 1960 the Maunsell 2–6–0s were about the commonest type of engine seen on the line. (J.H.W. Kent)

112. Chilworth managed a footbridge, which was useful when the crossing gates were closed or when you had small boys to entertain with the experience of looking down the engine's chimney. The Mogul this time is no. 31797, a rebuilt River class 2–6–4 tank, working a through train to the Western Region in October 1959 and going fast down the long bank from Gomshall to Shalford. (J.H.W. Kent)

113. Shalford station was another little gem on the Redhill-Guildford line, with an arcade under the main gable and a tall clustered chimney. Once again the wooden parcels shed is a sad let-down and the footbridge also could have been less aggressively modern. The combination of wheel barrow and porter's barrow on the grassy platform is unusual; not so no. 31866 on a down train to Guildford. (J.H.W. Kent)

114. Signalman Hill on duty in Shalford box on 24th October 1959. For this busy line the block instruments are all SR standard three position type, with everything in sight polished and gleaming. (J.H.W. Kent)

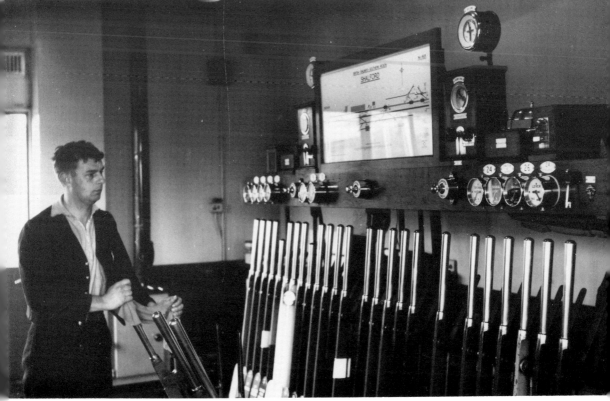

115. This picture of a train from Redhill arriving at Guildford allows us to see right through the engine shed, though 'train spotters' will have found it difficult to record many engine numbers as they swept by. Their engine in April 1955 is D1 class no. 31509. The local Permanent Way gang have been busy with the whitewash on the end of every rail or board in the layout, to make them more visible at night.

116. Another view from Farnham Road bridge, showing the station when there were still water cranes on the platforms. When Reading engine shed turntable was out of action occasionally, the M7 class 0–4–4 tanks were used on the trains to Redhill. No. 30246 has a curious Trio set, with a 'birdcage' at the far end but none this end.

117. Until the electrics came, Aldershot was connected with Ash on the Guildford-Reading line by a shuttle train which, headed by an M7 tank, is waiting in the bay platform. The train hauled by K10 class no. 394 is bound for Reading and is composed of an LBSCR 3-coach set by the elder Billinton.

(Lens of Sutton)